# Steam in West Cheshire

## and the North Wales Border

# Steam in West Cheshire

# and the North Wales Border

ACTON BRIDGE

# S D Wainwright

LONDON

IAN ALLAN LTD

First published 1981

ISBN 0 7110 1141 9

© Ian Allan Ltd 1981

Published by Ian Allan Ltd, Shepperton, Surrey;
and printed by Ian Allan Printing Ltd at their works
at Coombelands in Runnymede, England

# Introduction

Back in the days when there were about 20,000 steam locomotives at work in this country, people used to say to me, 'What on earth makes you want to photograph trains?' Well, some people take up photography and then look around for something to point the camera at whereas with me, the opposite was the case. I have been interested in railways and the steam locomotive in particular for as far back as I can remember and it was to record local railway activities that I got interested in photography.

Like most people I started off with a box type camera with its usual limitations of only being able to record static subjects on bright days. However, a friend of mine had at the time a Zeiss Ikonta camera together with a far greater knowledge of photography than I had and I asked him one day if he could photograph a moving train. 'Can't say I've ever tried' my friend replied, 'but I will see what I can do'. Seeing that we were at the time near to the railway by Saltney junction, we did not have to wait long before a train came by and my pal having already set the shutter to the fastest speed duly took aim and fired. Sufficent to say that a few days later I was presented with a very nice print of an LMS Compound and was well and truly 'hooked', deciding there and then that I must have a go at this myself.

Now this proved at the time to be easier said than done. World War 2 was not all that long over and the only cameras around which would do the job were second hand, of doubtful reliability and outrageous in price. However soon after I started to look around, the optical firm of Ross-Ensign introduced its 'Selfix' range of roll film cameras and one of the first models was a 16 on 120 version with a four element lens. I rather liked the look of this as it was very similar to the one my friend used so I went out and bought one for the then equivalent of three weeks' wages.

From this time onwards I only used roll film cameras with Compur type blade shutters for my railway photography. I did however, eventually change over to the square shaped negative for the following reason. I found that when photographing at ground level with an oblong format camera I always seemed to get too much foreground and not enough sky. The square negative gave me more height and enabled me to compose the picture a bit at the enlarging stage.

Film or the lack of it was another problem at the end of the 1940s. Most of it was still of the orthochromatic variety and when Ilford HP3 panchromatic film with a speed of 200 ASA appeared, it was regarded as revolutionary. However all these little snags were overcome and I continued to photograph trains in the Cheshire, Shropshire and North Wales area until steam was phased out in 1968, eventually finishing up with a collection of about 3,000 negatives.

Now this may not seem to be an enormous number for the period of time in question, but hours of work meant that picture taking was usually confined to weekends and holidays so, with spare time a bit limited, I tended to head for familiar places where rail traffic was heavy whenever I had the chance. I have in consequence little record of the branch lines, some of which were excellent from a pictorial point of view but carried very little traffic. So when the sun shone and I had time to spare, it was the main lines I made for with the prospect of a train every five minutes or so.

Considering the wide variety of steam motive power to be seen in this part of the country, I am always surprised that Chester and the surrounding area received so little attention from railway photographers. My favourite place for taking photographs was the half mile or so of the four track main line from the River Dee bridge outside Chester to the junction at Saltney where the Western Region lines branched off to the south. The Western Region boundary was actually about mid-way between the junction signalbox and Saltney station and from north to south the tracks were up and down main and up and down relief. They lay in a wide deep cutting which was crossed more or less in the centre by a high brick built bridge which carried a footpath across to the golf course on the north side. There were crossovers at Saltney connecting the fast and relief lines but as these were on the Welsh side of the turn off to the Western, any train bound for the Western Region had to use the relief lines from Chester No 6 signalbox onwards.

The variety of motive power to be seen here in steam days was phenomenal and it was rare to see the length on weekdays without at least one train in sight. Chester General station was joint LMS and GWR so most types of ex-Great Western engines with the exception of the 'Kings' could be seen together with a wide selection of ex-London,

Midland & Scottish and British Rail standard types.

The 'Kings' incidentally, were not allowed north of Saltney junction in Great Western and BR steam days and in practice rarely ventured north of Shrewsbury.

This piece of railway was one of the few in the country where two trains both going to London could pass each other going in opposite directions, an LMR one from North Wales to Euston and a WR train from Birkenhead to Paddington which had reversed at Chester. It was also the first place that I was granted a lineside walking permit for and I certainly put it into good use.

In my early picture days, Stanier Pacifics were a rarity at Chester, so quite often I would take a trip across to Crewe which was the nearest place to see these engines as a rule.

Now Crewe station was a veritable mecca for photographers and observers. The north end was spanned by a footbridge which was usually crammed to capacity with people on Saturday afternoons until

*Below:* 'King' class locomotives did not normally run north of Shrewsbury in regular service. On 29 September 1962 however, No 6000 *King George V* was used to haul a Talyllyn Railway Society special from Paddington to Ruabon and is shown passing Ruabon goods yard at the end of its run.

a ban was imposed on all spotters. One of the snags at Crewe was that due to the provision of low level goods awaiting lines from the south side at Basford Hall to both the Manchester and Scottish lines, few goods trains could be seen from the station area itself. Another hazard was the sheer size of the place. It was a good five minutes' walk from one end of the station to the other and successful picture taking was a matter of being in the right place at the right time. This could involve some rapid changes of viewpoint coupled with a knowledge of the timetable, the afternoon part of which I think I knew off by heart at one time.

Often by way of a change particularly if I felt like a trip on the 'Western' I would have a ride to Shrewsbury or Salop as it was universally referred to by railwaymen. This gave me a chance to photograph the 'Kings' which by 1960 had started to work regularly north of Wolverhampton, particularly on the down 'Cambrian Coast Express' on a round trip from London.

With three through platforms and four bays at the south end, Shrewsbury was a very busy compact place for the photographer. Like Chester, Shrewsbury station was 'joint' and most north to west trains changed engines here. Engines could also be seen on 'running in' turns after overhaul at Crewe works and all goods traffic passed through the station all of which gave a wide variety of subject matter for the camera. If I felt like an afternoon in the wilds of Cheshire, I used to head for a place called Acton Bridge situated on the West Coast main line about 14 miles north of Crewe.

Here I could photograph for a couple of hours with trains passing in both directions every five minutes or so on summer Saturdays, 'Lizzies', 'Scots', 'Jubilees', 'Patriots', followed one another in rapid succession. Speeds in the northerly direction were high as the line was downhill from Hartford to Weaver junction where the Liverpool trains branched off. Hazards here included the embankment setting on fire and odd bits of coal falling off tenders which had been over filled at Crewe. A lump of coal travelling at 80mph, plus,

could do some damage if it hit you and as regards burning embankments, I never stood anywhere where I could not get over the fence into the adjacent field if necessary, because if the grass went on fire on both sides of you, you were trapped!

Still, all good things come to an end and towards the end of steam on BR as standards of maintenance declined, I am afraid that my enthusiasm waned a bit. As a time served engineer I was brought up to understand that any machine worked better and was better to work on if it was kept clean. By 1968, the condition of most of the few steam locomotives still at work around here was to me an assault on the senses, so my railway photographic activities slowed down somewhat.

Now whilst I am still extremely interested in railways both full size and miniature and fully appreciate the power and efficiency of the diesel and electric locomotives which we see around these days, I am afraid that they do not have the magic for me that the steam engines did. I realise that to photograph modern motive power successfully needs a different approach than the style which was adopted for steam, particularly the three quarter front viewpoint which was the standard formula when I started. The modern idea is to use the train as part of an overall scene whereas the steam locomotive, particularly when working hard, was a subject in itself though one could hardly describe it as still life!

I still photograph railways, usually on the preserved lines and we get steam specials here at Chester each year which enables me to keep my hand in at the art, mostly now in the form of colour transparencies.

I enjoyed the time I spent photographing the iron horse and greatly regretted its passing like many other people. However steam railways have now become industrial archaeology so I am pleased to have been able to record some of Chester and district's railway history on film and hope that this small selection of my work will be of interest to people who remember steam engines at work as well as others who don't.

S. D. Wainwright
Blacon 1980

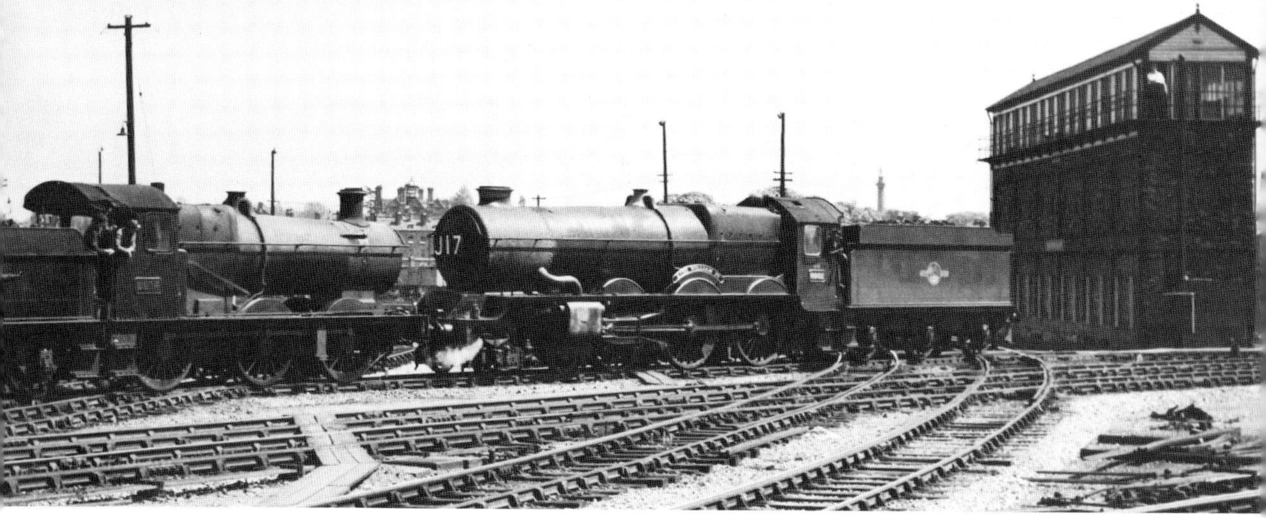
J17

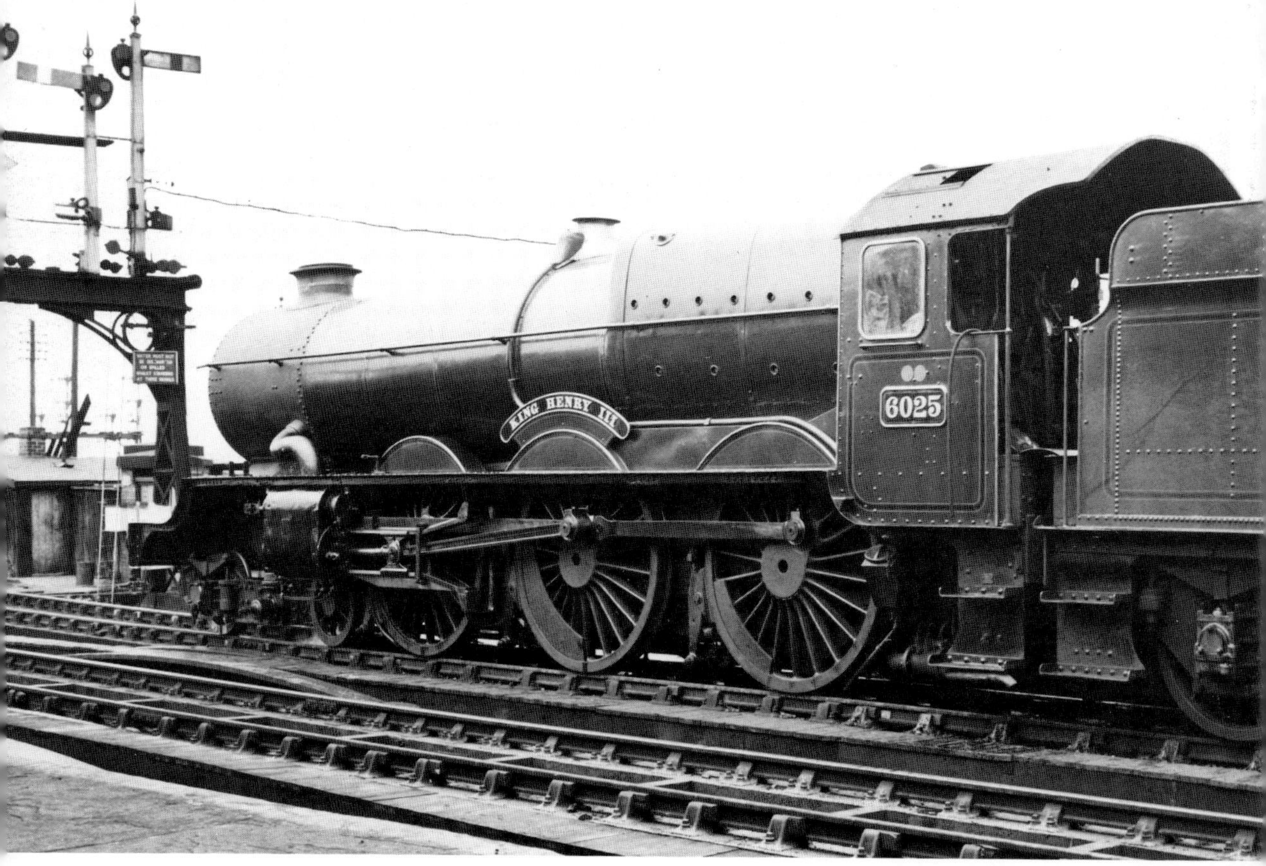
KING HENRY III
6025

*Left:* Having worked the down 'Cambrian Coast Express' from Paddington to Shrewsbury on 13 May 1961, No 6002 *King William IV* runs in reverse past Severn Bridge Junction signalbox coupled nose to nose with a Collett 0-6-0 No 2214 en route to Coleham shed for servicing.

*Below left:* On 11 June 1960 No 6025 *King Henry III* stands at the north end of Shrewsbury station at the end of a run with the northbound 'Cambrian Coast Express'. The notice on the gantry warns enginemen about spilling water whilst standing at the signals as it is likely to cascade into the street below.

*Below:* At Shrewsbury on 4 June 1960. No 6003 *King George IV* blowing off at the safety valves and making a lot of smoke backs slowly into Platform 7 to couple up to the 14.35 Birkenhead to Paddington express at the start of the second half of a round trip from London.

*Left:* Following its down working from London earlier in the day with the 'Cambrian Coast Express', No 6002 *King William IV* stands in Platform 7 at Shrewsbury on 13 May 1961 at the head of the 14.35 Birkenhead to Paddington express ready for the run back home.

*Below:* At the end of its run from London with the down 'Cambrian Coast Express', No 7030 *Cranbrook Castle* stands in Platform 4 at Shrewsbury station in April 1956. On the right, a Stanier Class 5 No 45060 waits in Platform 3 with a stopping train to Crewe.

*Right:* Hauled by No 7026 *Tenby Castle* the 11.10 Paddington to Birkenhead express passes Croes Newydd South Fork signalbox as it nears Wrexham on 13 June 1959. In the background one of the lightweight pannier tanks No 7443 can be seen shunting in Croes Newydd yard.

*Below right:* No 4079 *Pendennis Castle* is one of the better known members of its class and is now at the time of writing privately preserved in Australia. The engine is shown nearing Chester on 25 May 1957 with the morning parcels train from Greenford (London) to Chester.

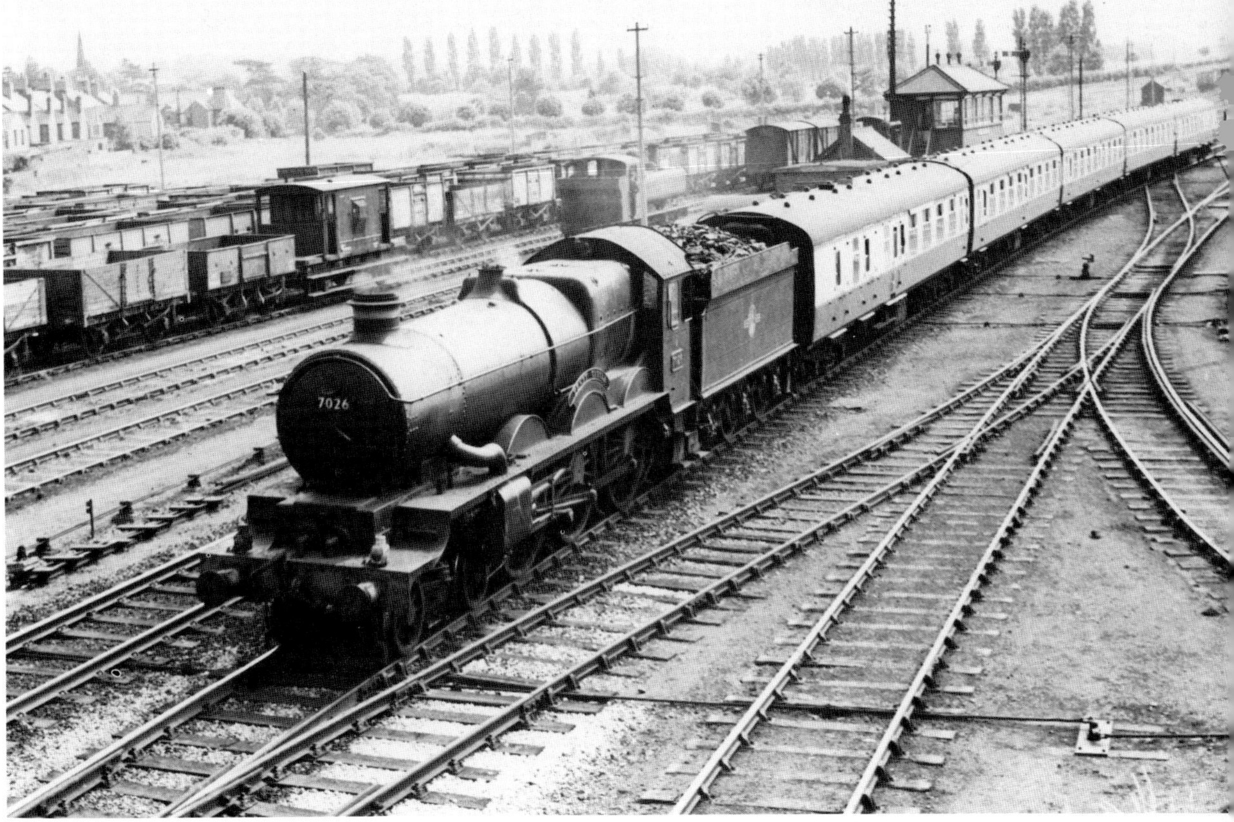
7026

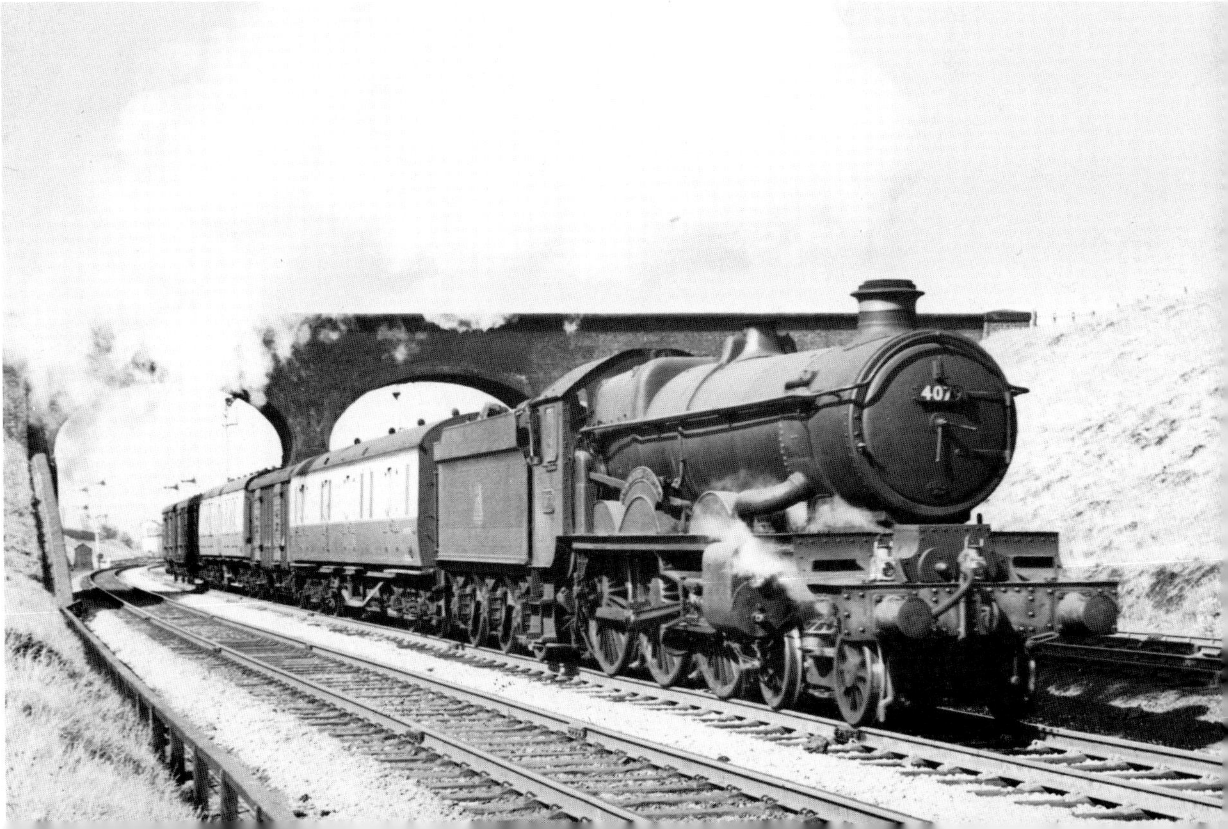

*Above:* Leaving Chester on 25 May 1957 'Castle' class No 5045 *Earl of Dudley* has just crossed the River Dee bridge and is entering the short deep cutting leading to Saltney Junction with the 08.45 Birkenhead to Paddington express.

*Below:* On a Saturday afternoon in June 1957 after working the 12.00 train from Shrewsbury to Chester No 5097 *Sarum Castle* backs the empty stock out of Chester General station to turn round on the triangular layout at the west end of the station before returning ECS to Shrewsbury.

*Above:* No 5033 *Broughton Castle* stands in Platform 2 at Chester General station on a summer afternoon in 1957 at the head of the 13.10 train from Birkenhead (Woodside) to Wolverhampton (Low Level). At the far end against the buffer stops can be seen the LMR 2-6-4T which has worked the train from Birkenhead.

*Below:* No 5026 *Criccieth Castle* sets off from Shrewsbury on 4 June 1960 with the 13.10 express from Paddington to Birkenhead. Another engine of the same class has just arrived at Platform 3 on the right with a train from Plymouth to Liverpool and Manchester while a Stanier Class 5 stands on the centre line with empty stock to form a stopping train to Crewe.

*Left:* At Chester General station on 17 March 1962 the fireman of ex-GW 4-6-0 No 4089 *Donnington Castle* looks back as his engine sets off for Wrexham with the 14.40 Birkenhead to London (Paddington) express. Note that the starting signals are still of L&NWR vintage.

*Below:* Headed by an unidentified 'Castle' class locomotive, the 11.55 express from Manchester (London Road) to Plymouth passes Severn Valley junction as it leaves Shrewsbury bound for its next stop at Hereford on 5 August 1960. Part of Coleham locomotive depot can be seen on the right including the ex-LNWR coaling shed by the rear of the train.

*Right:* With No 1022 *County of Northampton* in the lead, the 09.10 Paddington to Birkenhead express runs down the hill past Gresford station on a spring Saturday in 1955. Constant ground subsidence in this area caused by mining at the nearby colliery meant that a speed restriction of about 40mph was always in force on this stretch of line.

*Below right:* In fully lined out black livery which these engines carried in early BR days, No 1025 *County of Radnor* sets out from Chester past the No 6 signalbox on 8 September 1954 with the 18.20 stopping train to Wolverhampton Low Level composed of London Midland Region carriage stock.

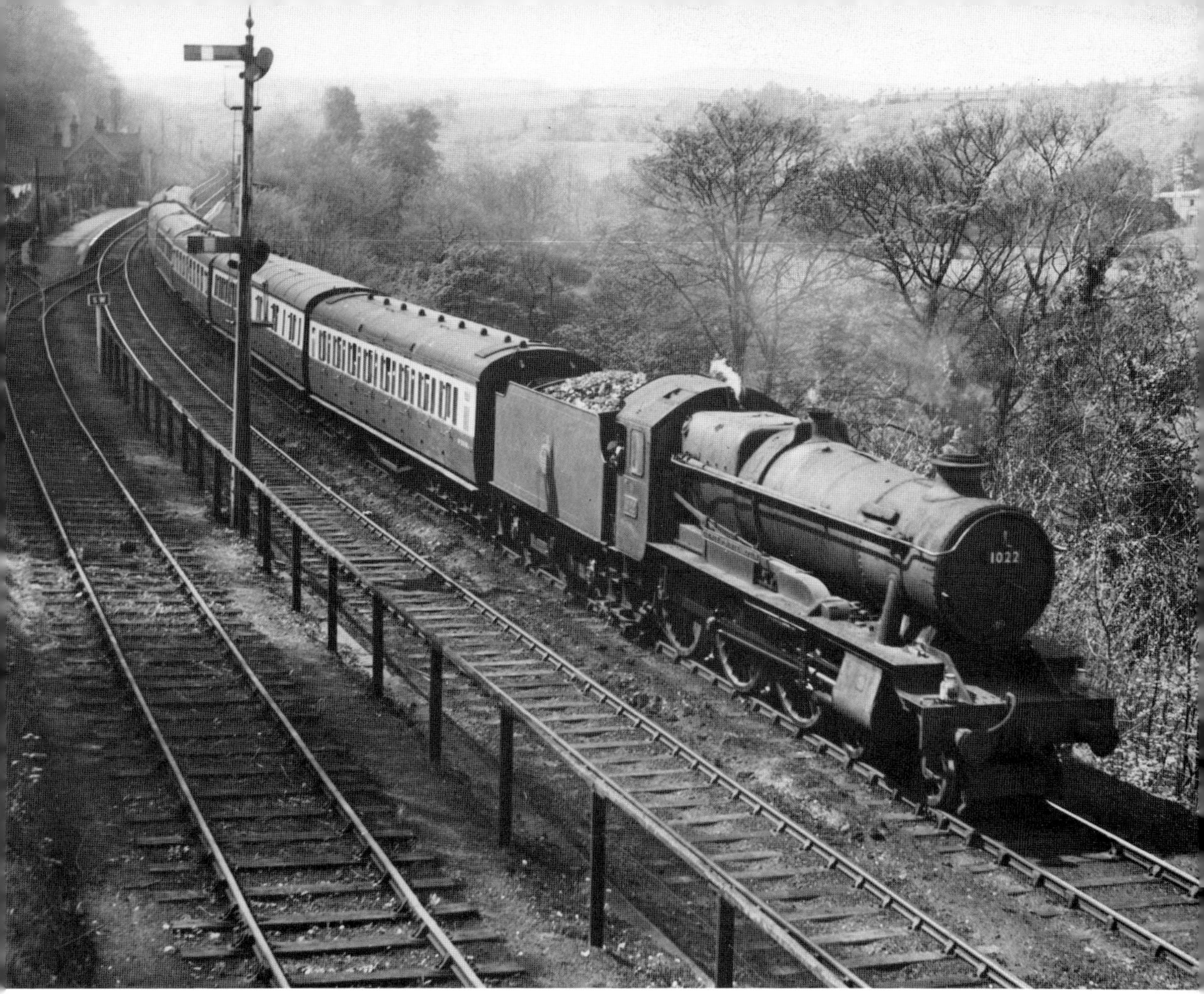
1022

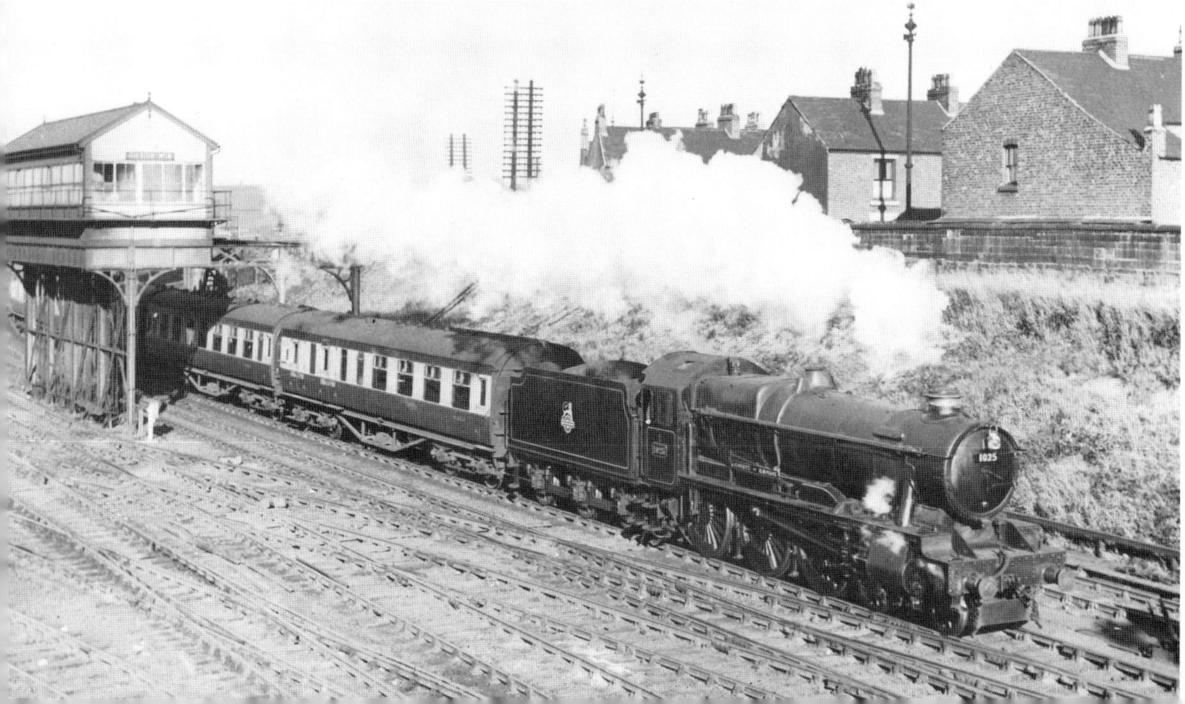
1025

*Above:* The 11.40 Birkenhead (Woodside) to Paddington express was always referred to locally as the 'Zulu' and included a restaurant car for the whole of the journey. The train is shown nearing Saltney station on 12 November 1955 hauled by No 1016 *County of Hants.*

*Below:* Pictured standing at the south end of Shrewsbury station on 2 August 1958 No 1016 *County of Hants* is shown finished in its later livery of lined out green and fitted with a double chimney which it is reputed improved the performance of the class enormously. It is a very hot day and both cab roof ventilators are open.

*Above:* On 29 September 1962 No 1013 *County of Dorset* passes Ruabon with a southbound express goods train. On the right No 7801 *Anthony Manor* coupled to No 7314 wait on the goods loop to take over a Talyllyn Railway Society special from London to Towyn (Merioneth) via the Llangollen branch.

*Below:* No 6916 *Misterton Hall* did not have to exert itself too much on the morning of 19 July 1958 when the Shrewsbury to Chester parcels train consisted of three vehicles only. The engine has acquired one of the narrow bodied Hawksworth pattern tenders which was built for use on the 'Modified Halls' from No 6971 onwards.

*Left:* The fireman of No 5927 *Guild Hall* has got the blower on hard as the engine stands in Platform 7 at Shrewsbury station at the head of the 12.10 relief express from Chester General to Birmingham Snow Hill on 16 May 1959. A young observer seems to be finding the footplate activity of more than usual interest.

*Below left:* The fireman of 'Modified Hall' No 6964 *Thornbridge Hall* takes it easy as the engine sets off from Shrewsbury at the head of the 16.50 stopping train to Chester on 2 August 1958. With the climb of Coton Hill starting just beyond the bridge in the background however, work with the shovel will soon commence.

*Top right:* Having worked from Paddington to Ruabon earlier in the day 'Modified Hall' No 6973 *Bricklehampton Hall* returns south double-heading No 5019 *Treago Castle* into Shrewsbury station with the 14.35 Birkenhead to Paddington express on 30 July 1960. On the left a BR Standard class 5 4-6-0 stands in the spare engine road waiting to back into the station on to a train for Crewe.

*Centre right:* With the city of Chester on the skyline 'Modified Hall' No 7900 *Saint Peter's Hall* crosses the River Dee bridge on 10 September 1960 with the 09.30 Birkenhead (Woodside) to Bournemouth (West) through train. On the left an express from the North Wales coast approaches Crane Street signalbox on the up fast line.

*Bottom right:* 'Modified Hall' No 6976 *Graythwaite Hall* blackens the evening sky as it approaches Rossett and the start of the four-mile climb to Gresford on 27 July 1963. The train is the 16.35 (Saturdays) express goods from Saltney Yard to Pontypool Road via Salop and Hereford.

*Left:* The driver of No 5971 *Merevale Hall* has noticed the camera as his engine accelerates the 14.35 Birkenhead to Paddington express past Croes Newydd North Fork towards its next stop at Ruabon on 25 March 1961. The track leading into the picture from the left is the Minera branch and also gives access to Croes Newydd locomotive shed.

*Below left:* Having backed off shed at Chester General station on 28 March 1959, No 4912 *Berrington Hall* moves forward towards the opposite side of the station ready to work the 13.50 stopping train to Wolverhampton (Low Level).

*Right:* On a Saturday morning in April 1957, 4-6-0 No 6944 *Fledborough Hall* nears Chester after its last stop at Saltney with the 10.15 train from Wellington (Salop). The engine is still painted in its first BR livery of lined out black with polished safety valve cover and copper capped chimney.

*Below:* The 'Granges' were regarded as one of the most versatile classes of ex-GWR engines and could be found working almost all types of trains between Chester and Shrewsbury. One of the later members of the class No 6872 *Crawley Grange,* was pictured on 29 September 1962 heading northwards past Ruabon goods yard with a train of high capacity mineral wagons.

*Left:* Saltney junction on 15 June 1957 and No 6853 *Morehampton Grange* comes off the western lines with a Saturday morning relief train from Birmingham (Snow Hill) to Chester. The 'dolly' or ground signal in the foreground is for trains starting out of the siding on the extreme left and heading for Chester.

*Below left:* No 6826 *Nannerth Grange* runs into platform 3 at Chester General on Sunday 21 July 1963 with the 16.22 train from Shrewsbury to Birkenhead (Woodside). Seeing that this is the end of the journey for the 'Grange', it shouldn't really be blowing off at the safety valves.

*Right:* After making the customary slow descent of Gresford bank with its various speed restrictions No 6833 *Calcot Grange* picks up speed through Rossett on 27 July 1963 with the 12.10pm express from Paddington to Birkenhead. The goods yard and loop lines were still in use at this date but the north signalbox had been demolished.

*Below right:* No 7802 *Bradley Manor* approaches Oswestry on 8 August 1962 with the 16.10 train from Whitchurch (Salop) to Welshpool. On the right are the ex-Cambrian Railways Locomotive, Carriage and Wagon Works and in the distance can be seen the motive power depot with a collection of ex-LMS Class 2MT 2-6-0s.

*Above:* The 16.10 Whitchurch (Salop) to Welshpool train runs past Ellesmere goods yard and signalbox into the station on 8 September 1962 headed by No 7803 *Barcote Manor*. On the left can be seen the picking up and setting down posts for the single line tokens for the section Ellesmere to Bettisfield.

*Below:* The south end of Shrewsbury station on 31 July 1963 and the area has now been tidied up a little after the work involved in providing three through tracks between Platforms 3 and 4 at this end of the station. No 7818 *Granville Manor* is shown running into Platform 4 from Aberystwyth with the up 'Cambrian Coast Express'.

*Above:* In the usual superb condition which Aberystwyth kept its top link engines No 7802 *Bradley Manor* sets off from Shrewsbury for Aberystwyth with the down 'Cambrian Coast Express' on 16 May 1959. The pilot engine is No 7330, one of the last series of 2-6-0 with side window cab which were only allowed on the Mid-Wales line after modifications to reduce the axle loading to bring them in line with the rest of the class.

*Below:* The first of its class ex-GWR 4-6-0 No 7800 *Torquay Manor* was based at Chester for a period in the mid-1950s. The engine is pictured nearing Saltney junction on 31 March 1956 with a mixed goods train from Chester bound for the Western Region.

*Above:* On the evening of 5 August 1961 the 12.30 Pwlleli to Birkenhead train headed by No 7828 *Odney Manor* runs past Croes Newydd towards its next stop at Wrexham. The old wooden armed signal on the right governs the exit from the down goods loop and seems to have lost the upper half of the ring which indicates that it is a siding signal.

*Below:* 'Star' class No 4061 *Glastonbury Abbey* runs into Shrewsbury station from the Wellington line with a train of empty stock to form a stopping train to Chester in May 1956. The engine which was nearing the end of its days of service, had been used on a number of enthusiast specials about this time which was the reason for the GW style numerals on the buffer beam.

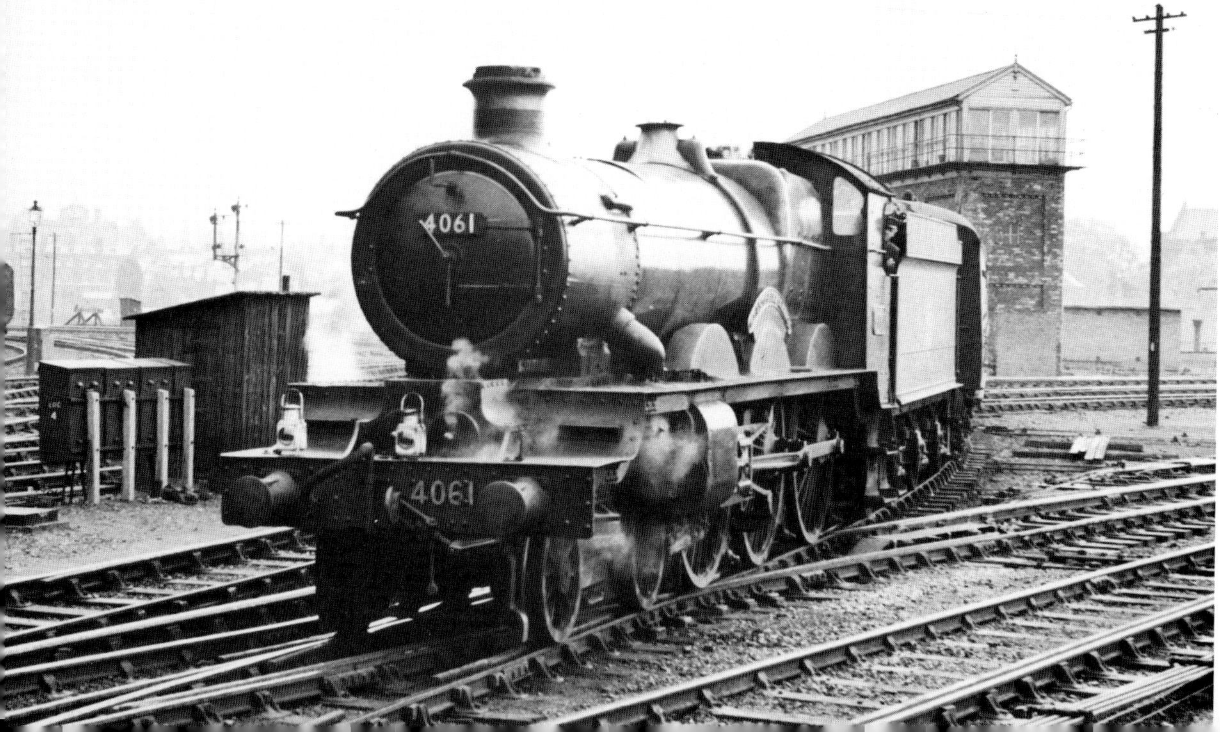

*Above:* In 1957 No 3440 *City of Truro* was restored to working order at Swindon after being preserved for some years at the Railway Museum at York and was widely used on enthusiast specials. Pictured at Ruabon on 31 March of that year the veteran takes a breather before returning to Shrewsbury light engine after working a Festiniog Railway Society special from Wolverhampton.

*Below:* On Sunday 4 April 1965 Croes Newydd shed (Wrexham) still has ex-GW locos on the strength despite London Midland Region control. No 6625 is shown standing on the coal stage line with a Stanier 2-8-0 No 48325 and pannier tank No 9610. Another two 0-6-2Ts are in the shed on the right and a BR Standard 2-6-4T is in the left background.

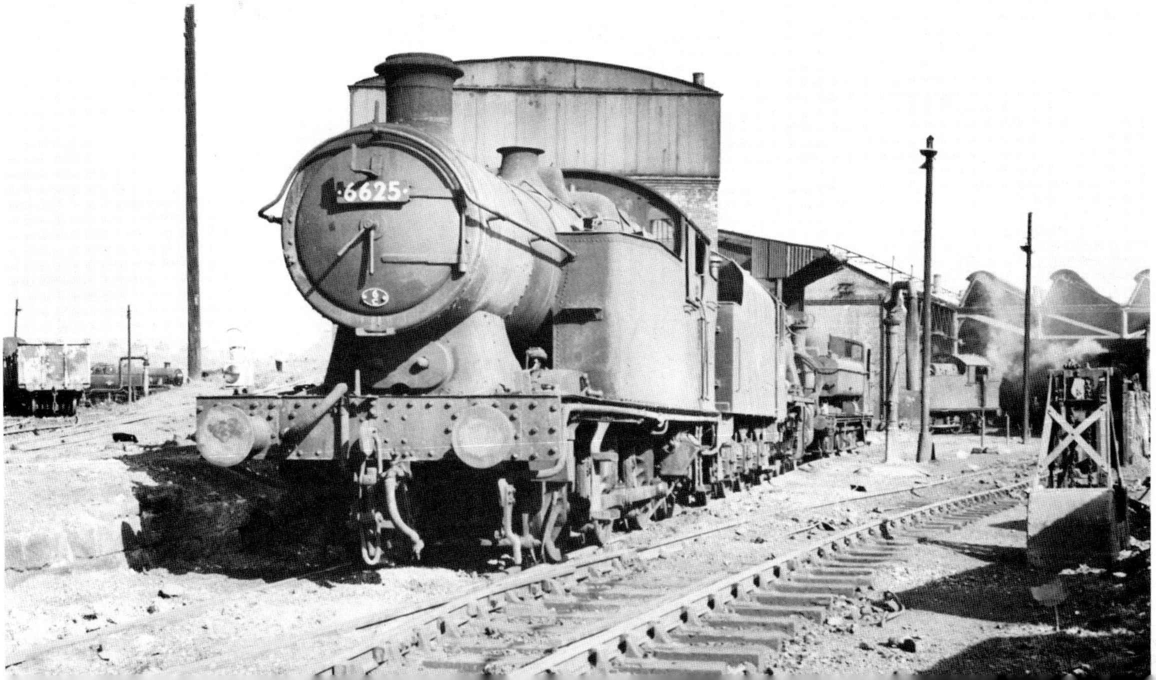

*Above:* With the gradients predominantly downhill, it did not take much effort on the part of an engine to get from Wrexham to Saltney Yard. With steam shut off 2-8-0 No 3827 drifts down the slight incline from Pulford level crossing to Balderton on 19 July 1958 with a train of tank wagons bound for Ellesmere Port.

*Below:* Heading towards Coton Hill Yard from the Wellington line, 2-8-0 No 3860 passes through Shrewsbury station along the centre road with a down goods train on 6 September 1963. The engine is one of the later series of 2-8-0 built from 1938 onwards to the original Churchward design but with detail differences including side window cabs, fire iron casings and modified motion brackets.

*Above:* The climb up to the junction from Saltney Yard seems to have livened up the fire on 2-8-0 No 3817, seen heading towards Chester in rather grimy condition on 24 September 1960 with a train of tank wagons bound for Ellesmere Port.

*Below:* The larger wheeled ex-GW 2-6-2Ts were not usually to be found on passenger trains between Chester and Shrewsbury. Here however No 4103 is seen heading the 08.35 Birmingham (Snow Hill) to Chester train round the curve from Saltney station to the junction on a day in the summer of 1954.

*Above:* Ex-GW 2-6-2T No 5174 comes from Saltney Yard past the junction and heads towards Chester with a mixed goods train on 15 June 1957. The buffer stop on the left could do with renewal by the looks of it. All that remains of the beam is the tie bar between the two uprights.

*Left:* Shedded at Chester at the time the photograph was taken, ex-GW 2-6-0 No 4377, one of the original series of 2-6-0 now fitted with outside steam pipes and a short safety valve cover heads out from Chester towards Saltney in August 1955 with a loose coupled goods train.

*Above:* Fitted with a Churchward intermediate pattern 3,500gal capacity tender, ex-GW 2-6-0 No 6339 climbs towards its next stop at Gresford from Rossett on 12 September 1959. The train is the 12.30 (Saturdays only) from Birkenhead (Woodside) to Ruabon and with the air hot and humid, little exhaust can be seen coming from the chimney.

*Right:* With a top speed of at least 70mph the '43xx' class of ex-GW 2-6-0s could usually be relied on to give a reasonable performance with lightly loaded express trains. In what looks to be top condition, No 5369 was seen on 19 July 1958 working the 09.45 Saturdays only relief express from Chester to Shrewsbury between Balderton and Pulford siding.

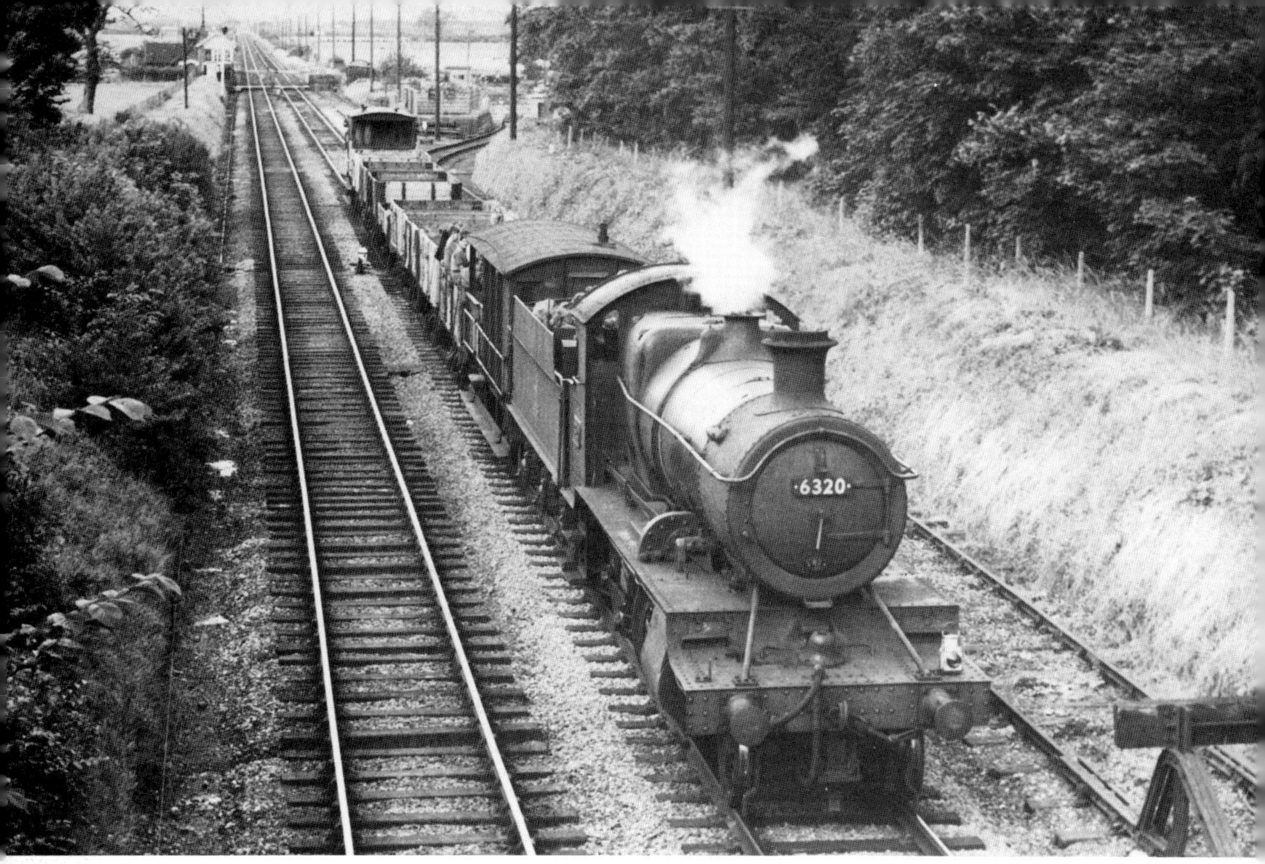
6320

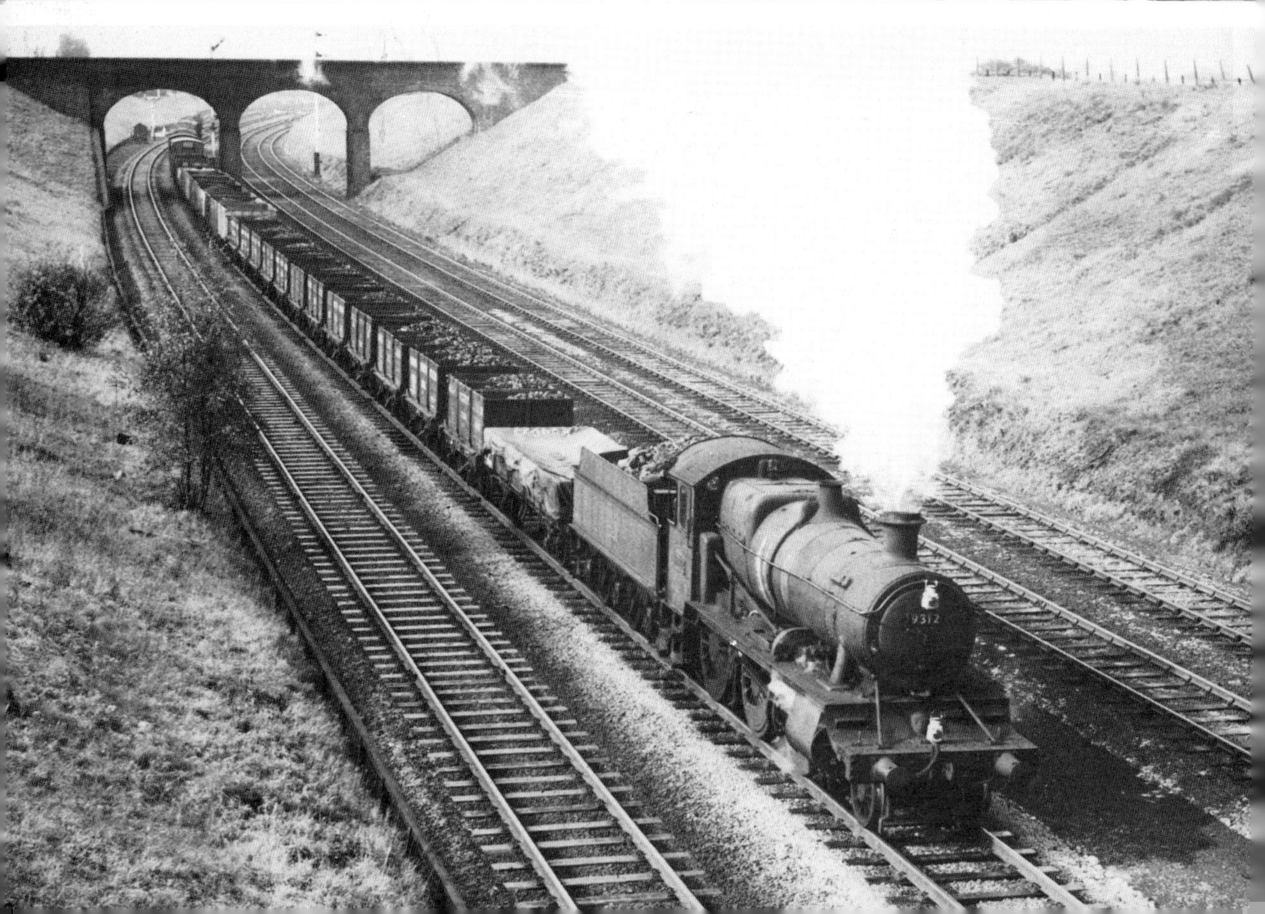
9312

*Above left:* On 1 August 1958 2-6-0 No 6320 heads past Balderton in the direction of Wrexham with a train loaded with track material and a working party travelling rough on the first wagon. Balderton station which closed in 1948 was situated just beyond the level crossing gates in the background and the terminus of the Duke of Westminster's 15in gauge railway from Eaton Hall was in the goods yard to the right of the rear brake van.

*Left:* 2-6-0 No 9312 runs through the cutting from Saltney junction towards Chester on 20 September 1957 with a mixed goods train bound for Birkenhead. The 12 special open container wagons near the front of the train carry Monk's Ferry steam coal and can be unloaded direct into ships' bunkers.

*Above:* With the air full of smoke, photography in engine sheds could be a tricky business. Here in rather murky conditions and near the end of its working life, 2-6-0 No 6301 rests inside Croes Newydd shed on a Sunday afternoon 7 October 1962.

*Above:* Still active in Birkenhead Docks in the summer of 1955, '2021' class 0-6-0PT No 2160 lurches its way round one of the many sharp curves in an area known as the Four Bridges. What the red flag in the ground by the rear of the engine signified was anyone's guess. Certainly no notice was being taken of it.

*Below:* Apart from the two different types of cab, there were few detail differences between the various members of the '57xx' class of pannier tanks. However No 8727 which was pictured on Croes Newydd shed on 21 June 1959, seems to have acquired its tanks second hand off a much older engine as they are constructed with snap head rivets instead of the usual flush or countersunk variety.

*Above:* With a top speed of about 60mph the '57xx' pannier tanks were quite useful engines on local passenger work. No 9752 was photographed passing Croes Newydd North Fork, Wrexham, on 25 March 1961 with the 15.45 stopping train from Wrexham (General) to Llangollen.

*Below:* On the afternoon of 20 June 1959, pannier tank No 8709 of the earlier series with older type cab hauls a transfer goods train from Saltney Yard to Chester into the cutting towards the River Dee bridge. The train seems to comprise a wide variety of rolling stock including some ferry vans.

*Left:* The '16xx' class of pannier tank always found useful employment in the Oswestry area by reason of their light axle loading and although not introduced until 1949 in BR days, they were a GW design. No 1668 is pictured at Oswestry on 8 August 1962 with an old clerestory coach in the background in engineering department use.

*Top right:* After visiting Mold junction LMR shed on a day in the summer of 1954. Ex-GW 2-8-0 No 4708 is taken back to Chester out of steam and propelled by an ex-LMS Stanier 2-6-4T. '47xx' 2-8-0s were rarely seen in the Chester area, although night-time express goods trains between London and Birkenhead were a regular turn for this class of engine at one period.

*Centre right:* Apart from the safety valve cover, whistles and top feed, the '30xx' class of ex-GW 2-8-0 were virtually identical to the LNER Class 04. Still active in August 1956, No 3016 accelerates a train of hopper wagons from Saltney towards Chester. This class of engine was not vacuum fitted which explains the lack of pipework on the front buffer beam.

*Left:* Ellesmere station (Salop) on 8 September 1967 and ex-GW 0-4-2 auto tank No 1432 has just arrived with the 17.05 train from Wrexham (Central). This was the last day that the branch line via Bangor on Dee was open for passenger traffic, hence the larger than usual number of passengers and the photographers.

*Right:* The Talyllyn Railway Society's special trains from London (Paddington) to Towyn usually provided something out of the ordinary in the way of motive power. Pictured waiting to take over the train at Ruabon for its journey onward to Towyn on 26 September are privately owned 2-6-2T No 4555 and No 7827 *Lydham Manor* which at this time was still running in BR ownership.

*Above:* A rare visitor to Shrewsbury on 16 April 1960 was a Pontypool Road based 2-8-2T No 7246 shown passing through the station with a northbound goods train bound for Coton Hill yard. With only room for 2,500gal of water in the engine's tanks, a few stops for replenishment purposes must have been made on the run from Hereford.

*Below:* After a run light engine from Oswestry Ex-GW 0-6-0 No 3200 pauses by the signalbox at Ellesmere (Salop) on 8 September 1962 prior to carrying out a few shunting movements. Four different types of tender were used with this class of engine and this member is coupled to one of the Collett pattern tenders with 3,000gal water capacity.

*Above:* On a winter Saturday morning in 1955, a Collett 0-6-2T engine No 5647 climbs past Saltney junction with a Chester bound goods train. The air was very cold which provided clouds of condensing steam and numbed the photographer who thawed himself out by the signalbox stove afterwards.

*Below:* GW pannier tanks were still active in the Wrexham area in 1966. On 1 September of that year, No 9610 was pictured traversing Croes Newydd North Curve in the Minera direction with a train of mineral wagons. Along with other members of the class, the engine has had its cab number plates removed.

*Top:* The ex-Great Central Railway station at Wrexham was the start of the Cambrian Railway branch line to Ellesmere (Salop) via Bangor-on-Dee. With Wrexham parish church in the background 0-4-2 auto tank No 1432 was pictured on 8 September 1962 ready to start with the 18.35 train to Ellesmere. It is the last day of the passenger service hence the presence of the photographers.

*Above:* Another regular performer on the morning Wrexham to Chester auto was 0-4-2T No 1416, based at Croes Newydd and seen here propelling its train towards Chester from its last stop at Saltney. The car next to the engine is one of the Hawksworth variety built in BR days to a GW design.

*Right:* Oswestry goods yard on 8 August 1962 and 0-6-0 lightweight pannier tank No 1638 is busy carrying out some shunting work after arriving with a short goods train. This engine was ultimately preserved and is at the time of writing, working on the Dart Valley Railway in Devonshire.

*Below:* The 'Dukedogs' helped out on the Mid-Wales line until the end of their existence. Here on 5 August 1960 No 9017 coupled to No 7818 *Granville Manor* backs on to the down 'Cambrian Coast Express' in Platform 4 at Shrewsbury station prior to a double headed trip at least as far as Machynlleth. Here the train will divide, part going to Aberystwyth and the remainder to Pwllheli.

*Above:* At Oswestry on 8 August 1962 ex-GW 0-4-2T No 1438 runs towards the bay platform with the 16.59 auto train from Gobowen. On the right hand side No 1638 shunts in the yard with another engine of the same class performing similar duties on the far left. An ex-LMS 2-6-0 Class 2P stands in the station at the same time with the 17.25 train to Whitchurch.

*Left:* Hauling two vintage auto coaches, auto fitted ex-GW pannier tank No 6405 is shown nearing Saltney junction from Chester on a Saturday morning in April 1957 with the 11.05 train to Oswestry. A speed restriction is in force and the slower than usual pace causes the engine to blow off at the safety valves.

*Top:* Chester's ex-GW engine shed was a cramped awkward place to work in or to take pictures. Standing by the coaling stage on 18 July 1959 are pannier tank No 3676 coupled to 2-8-0 No 2845 and an Austerity 2-8-0. Flanked by running lines on one side and sidings on the other, the shed could only be reached by the footbridge just visible over the centre 2-8-0.

*Above:* For the last two years of its existence, the ex-Great Central Railway shed at Rhosddu (Wrexham) came under the control of the Western Region. Shown on shed there on Sunday 21 June 1959 are 0-6-2T No 6610, ex-LMS 2-6-2T No 40126, 0-6-0 pannier tanks Nos 1669 and 1618 plus a couple of BR Standard Class 3, 2-6-2Ts Nos 82037 and 82021.

*Above:* After the ex-GW shed at Chester closed in April 1960, Western Region engines were serviced at the city's ex-LMS shed. Recognisable in the picture taken on Sunday 11 September 1960 are from the left BR Standard Class 4 75051, 'Castle' class No 5059 *Earl St Aldwyn*, No 5944 *Ickenham Hall*, No 5948 *Siddington Hall*, and an ex-LMS 0-6-0T.

*Left:* Fitted with Caprotti valve gear, British Rail Standard Class 8P 3-cylinder 4-6-2 No 71000 *Duke of Gloucester* was the only example of its class to be built. The engine was photographed at Crewe on 19 August 1957 backing out of No 2 bay after working a stopping train from Shrewsbury via Whitchurch.

*Below left:* Still running unnamed in September 1956, 'Britannia' class 4-6-2 No 70046 makes a very gentle start from Chester with the down 'Irish Mail'. The engines of this class shedded at Holyhead including the one shown were fitted with tenders having an increased coal capacity to enable them to work from Euston with the boat trains, as the seven tons capacity of the smaller tenders was insufficient for the 264-mile journey.

*Above:* On a Sunday evening 24 May 1959, 'Britannia' class 4-6-2 No 70048 *The Territorial Army 1908-58* heads the 13.15 Euston to Holyhead, the 'Emerald Isle Express' through the cutting by Chester golf club on its nonstop run from Chester to Bangor. This was another train which was worked throughout by Holyhead engines.

*Below:* Chester General station on 17 August 1963 and 'Britannia' class 4-6-2 No 70027 *Rising Star* runs alongside Platform 4 to make its scheduled stop with the 11.55 Manchester (Exchange) to Holyhead express. The bay window at the left hand end of the footbridge is the No 3 signalbox which controls the crossovers in the middle of the station.

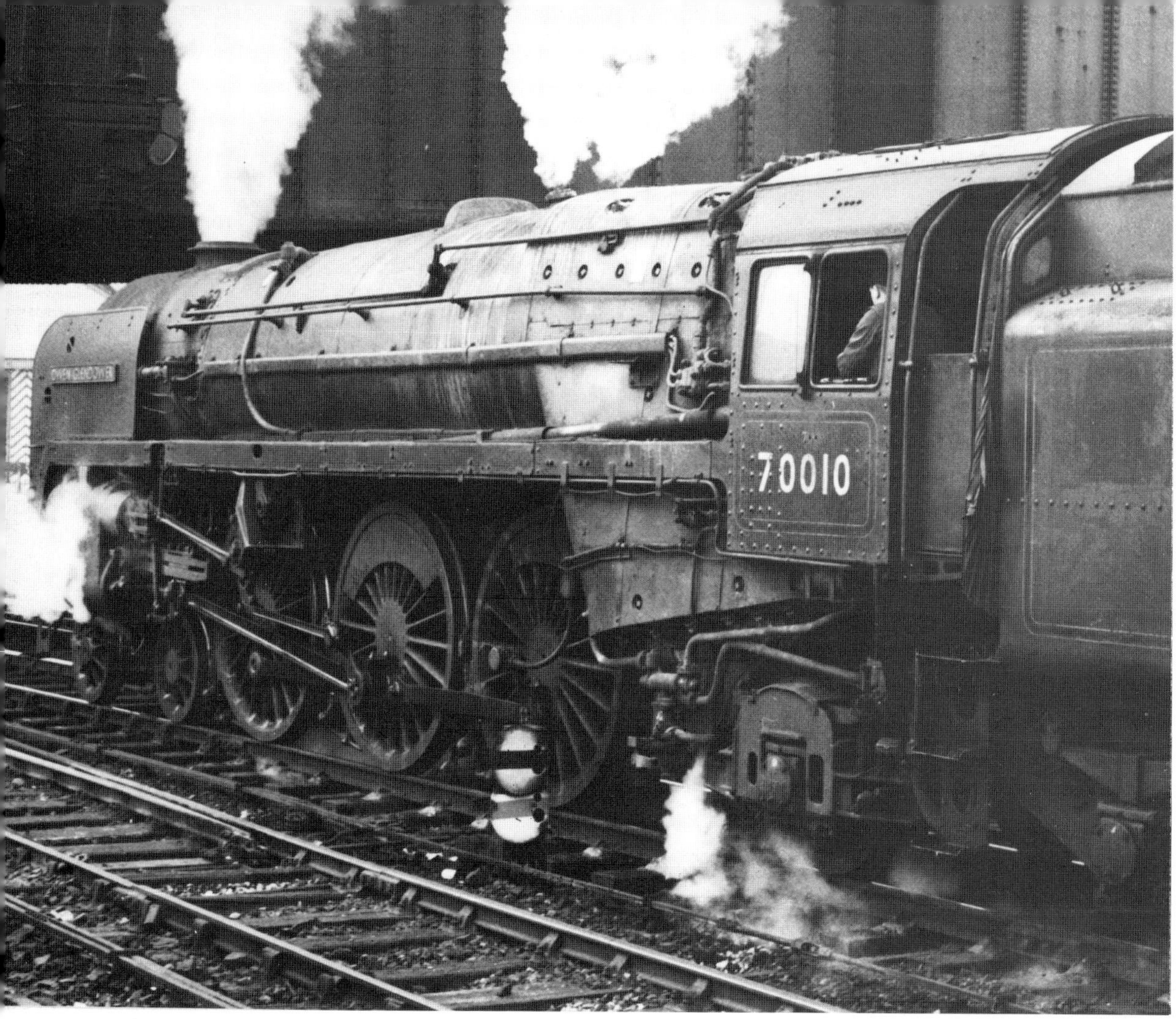
70010

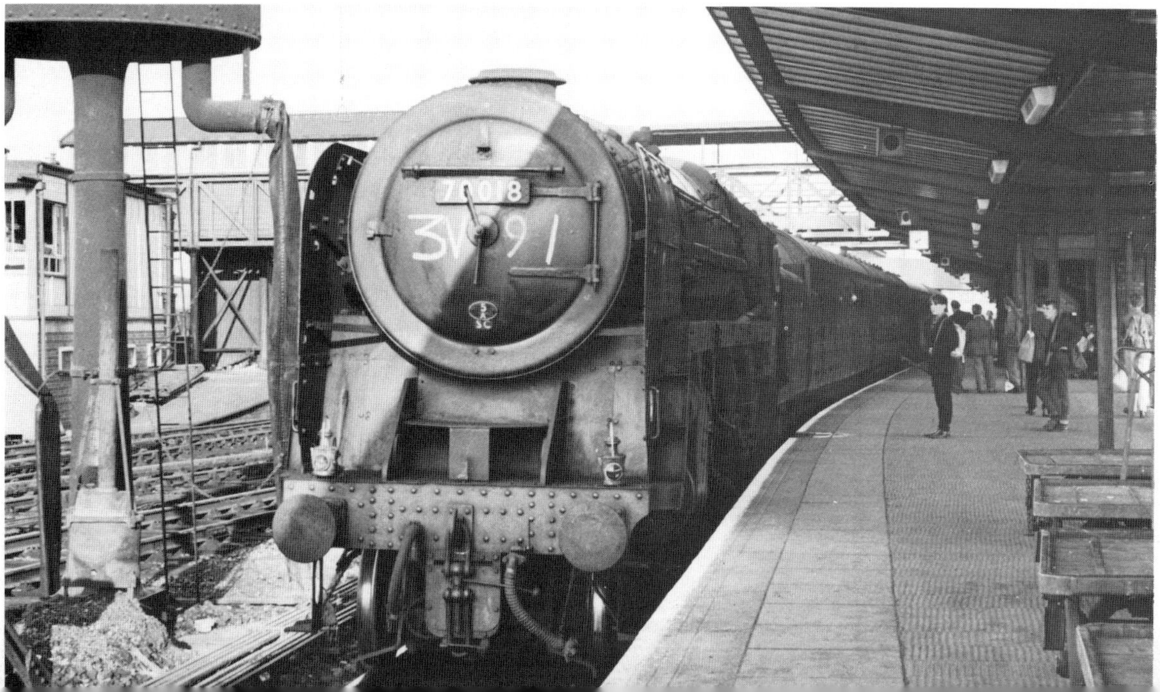
70018
3V91

*Left:* One of the main considerations when British Rail Standard steam locomotives were designed was ease of servicing and maintenance. This view of 'Britannia' class 4-6-2 No 70010 *Owen Glendower* at Chester on 5 June 1963 clearly shows the large amount of external pipework carried by these engines and also the regulator rod with its centre compensating lever on the outside of the boiler barrel above the handrail.

*Below left:* On a Sunday evening 9 June 1963 No 70018 *Flying Dutchman*, a 'Britannia' class 4-6-2, stands in Platform 4 at Chester General station with the 19.00 train from Crewe to Bangor. This engine was one of a number of the class which were first allocated to the Western Region, all eventually having the handrails removed from the smoke deflectors to give improved forward visibility from the cab.

*Right:* The 16.30 Manchester (Exchange) to Llandudno club train was usually hauled by a well turned out Stanier Class 5. A change from the normal took place on 2 September 1966 when BR Standard Class 5 No 73011 was photographed at the head of the train nearing Helsby junction.

*Below:* In August 1954 BR Standard Class 5 No 73041 was pictured between Connah's Quay and Shotton (Low Level) stations with the afternoon train from Holyhead to Birmingham (New St). This engine is running with one of the earlier pattern tenders fitted to this class, with inset bunker sides to give good visibility from the cab when running tender first.

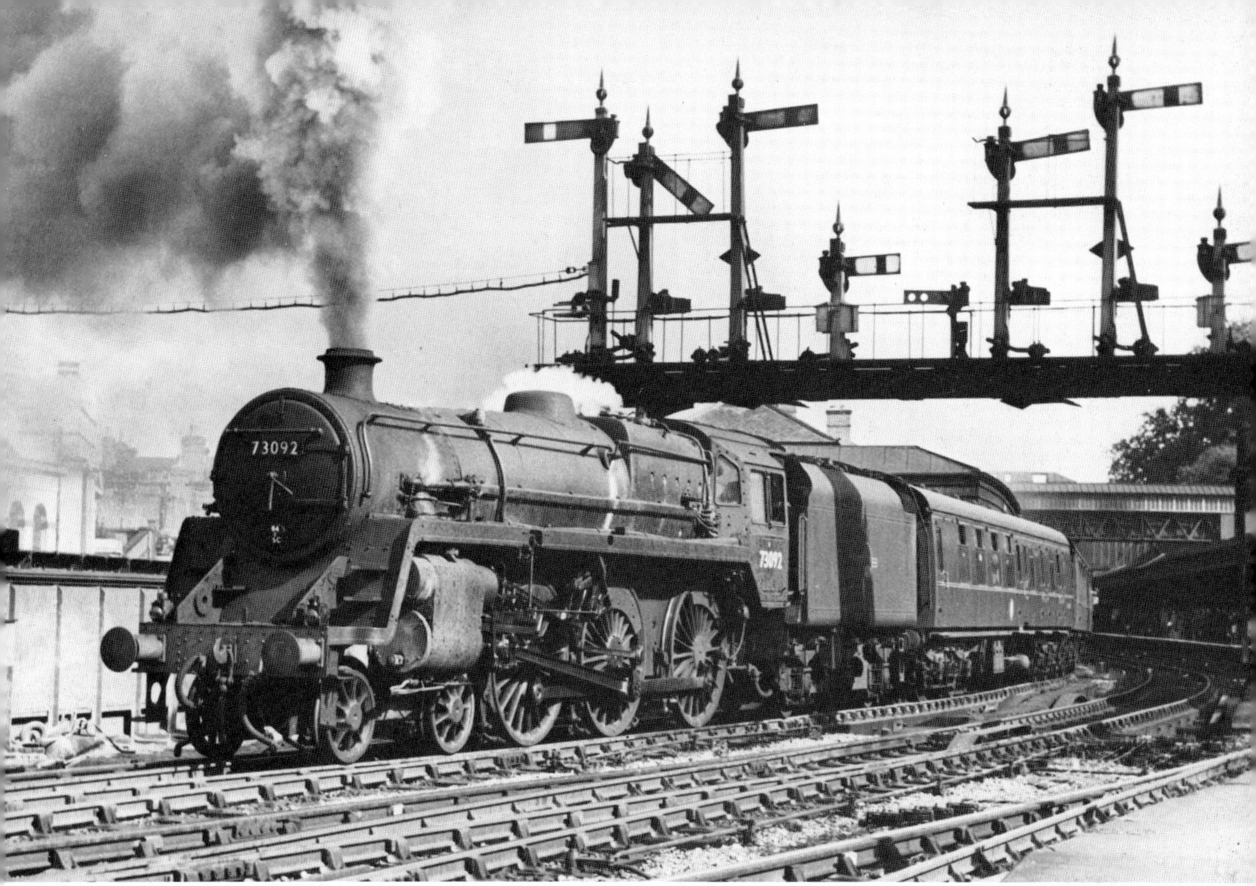
73092
73092

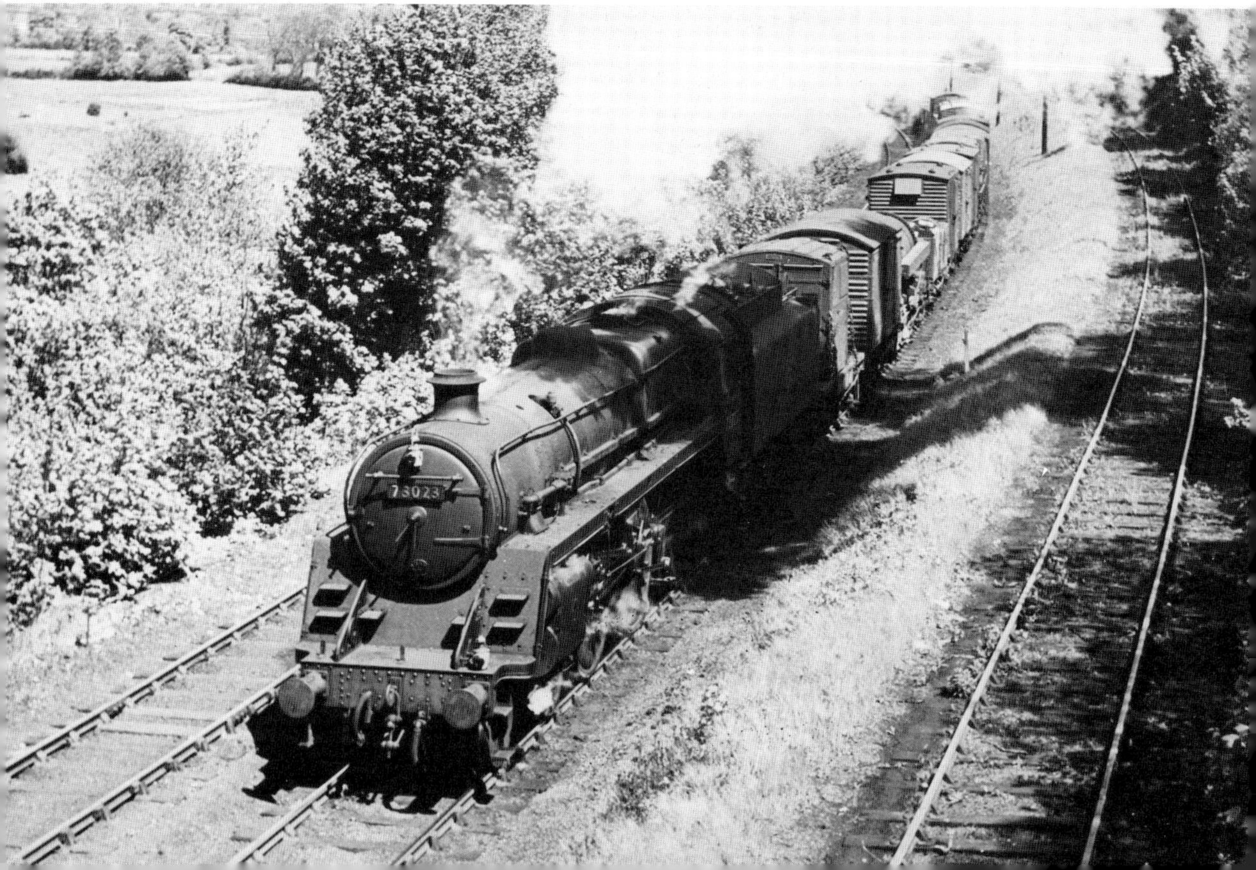
73023

*Above left:* Some of the BR Standard Class 5s allocated to the Western Region were painted in the lined out green passenger livery. One of these No 73092 is shown leaving Shrewsbury for Crewe on 30 July 1960 with the 06.00 Penzance to Manchester (London Road) through train. The engine is running with one of the later pattern tenders with larger coal capacity.

*Below left:* Chester Western Region shed had its allocation of BR Standard Class 5s and one of these No 73023 is shown climbing Gresford Bank in the spring of 1955 with a southbound express goods train. The line on the right of the picture is a goods refuge siding.

*Above:* In the winter schedules the engine that worked the 08.35 passenger train from Manchester (Exchange) to Chester returned home with an express goods train from Saltney yard to Patricroft. BR Standard Class 5 No 73038 is shown starting the second part of its day's work as it heads towards Chester in the spring of 1957.

*Below:* Following an incident on the north Wales coast line on 10 March 1956 BR Standard Class 4 4-6-0 No 75034 returns past Saltney junction towards Chester with the Chester LMR breakdown train. Note the two vintage coaches in the train used as riding vans for the breakdown gang.

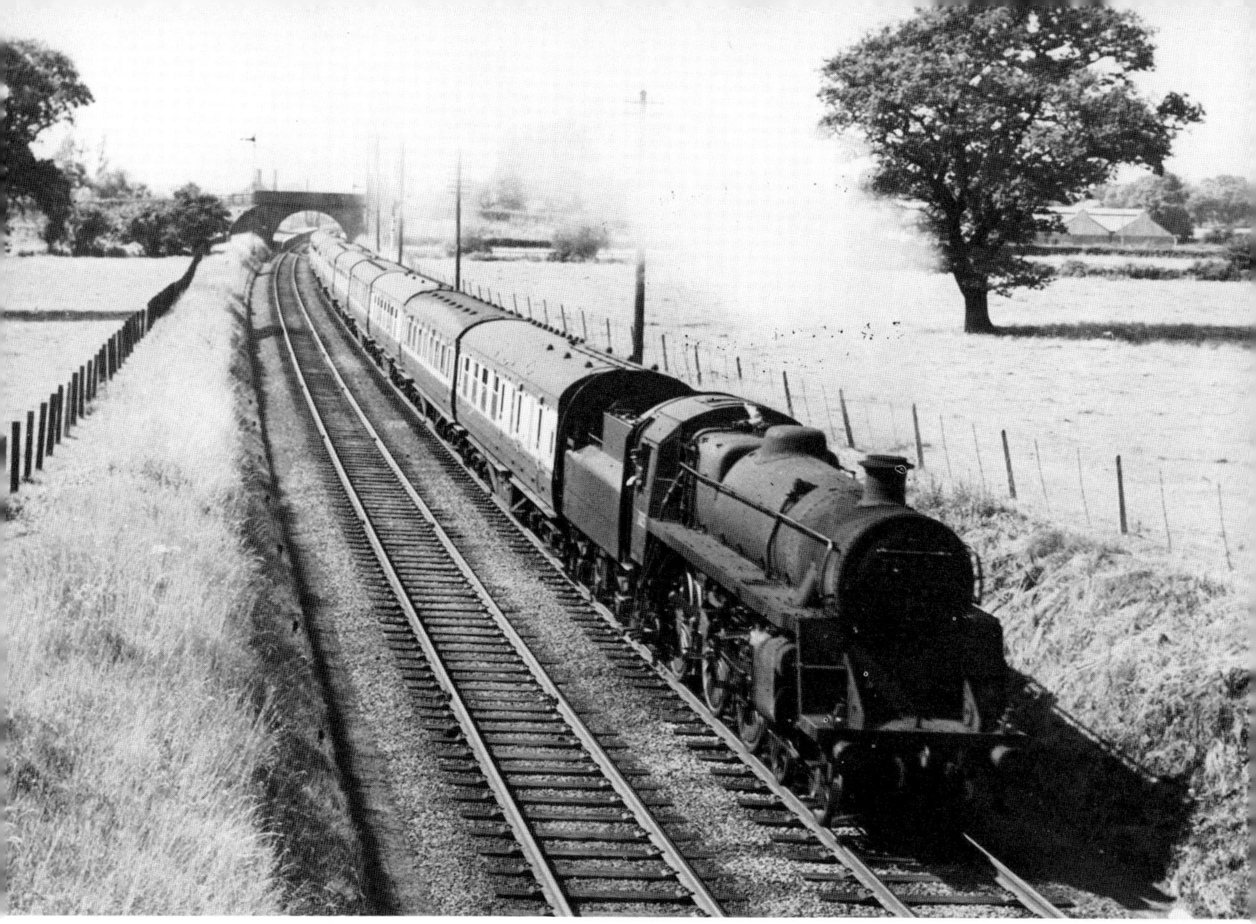

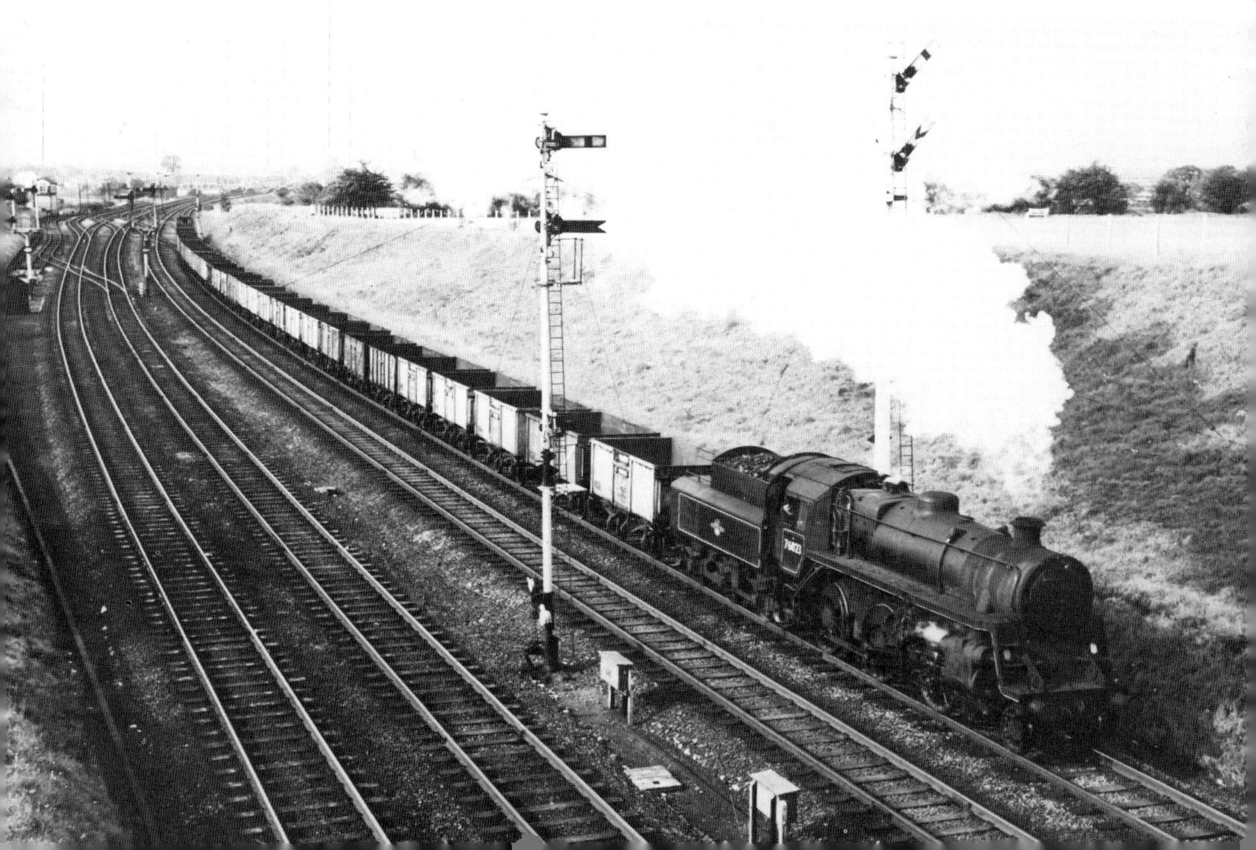

*Left:* Looking a bit neglected BR Standard Class 4 4-6-0 No 75035 heads past Waverton station between Chester and Crewe on an August Saturday in 1955 with an afternoon train from Llandudno to Birmingham (New Street). The engine must be steaming well despite its external condition as the fireman has time for a 'breather'.

*Below left:* The BR Standard Class 4 2-6-0s were not too common in the Chester area until the mid-1960s. However No 76023 was used to haul the morning train of empty coal wagons from Mold junction yard to the Midlands shown passing Saltney junction on 26 September 1961.

*Above:* Apart from a few minor details the BR Class 2 2-6-0 was very similar to the ex-LMS version and performed similar duties. On an August morning in 1955 No 78039 was photographed passing Saltney junction on the down fast line with a morning stopping train from Chester to Rhyl.

*Below:* Traversing the deep cutting between Saltney and the River Dee bridge BR Standard Class 4 2-6-4T No 80045 nears Chester with the 14.55 stopping train from Rhyl on 20 June 1959. Being a summer Saturday traffic is heavy and the normal load of three non-corridor coaches nearest to the engine has been increased by the addition of the five corridor coaches at the rear.

*Above:* Having traversed the Chester avoiding lines known as 'the cutting' from the direction of Hooton, an Austerity ex-WD 2-8-0 No 90173 crosses over to the down slow lines by Chester No 6 signalbox on 8 September 1954 with a train of tank wagons from Ellesmere Port bound for the Western Region lines at Saltney.

*Below:* Any train starting from Saltney Yard in a northerly direction was faced with a fairly steep gradient up to the junction with the last part after Saltney station on a sharp curve. An Austerity 2-8-0 No 90214 is pictured making very heavy going of it as it approaches the junction signalbox on 12 November 1965 with a goods train bound for Chester.

*Above:* Having completed the climb from Saltney Yard up to the junction on 25 February 1956 Austerity 2-8-0 No 90686 gets into its stride towards Chester. Note that the pony truck wheels at the front of the engine are of the solid pattern.

*Below:* On summer Saturdays it was a regular feature for ex-LNER 'B1' class engines to work passenger trains throughout from the Eastern Region to Llandudno. No 61163 was pictured getting into its stride towards Mold junction on a morning in 1954 hauling a very mixed selection of Eastern Region stock including some of Great Central ancestry.

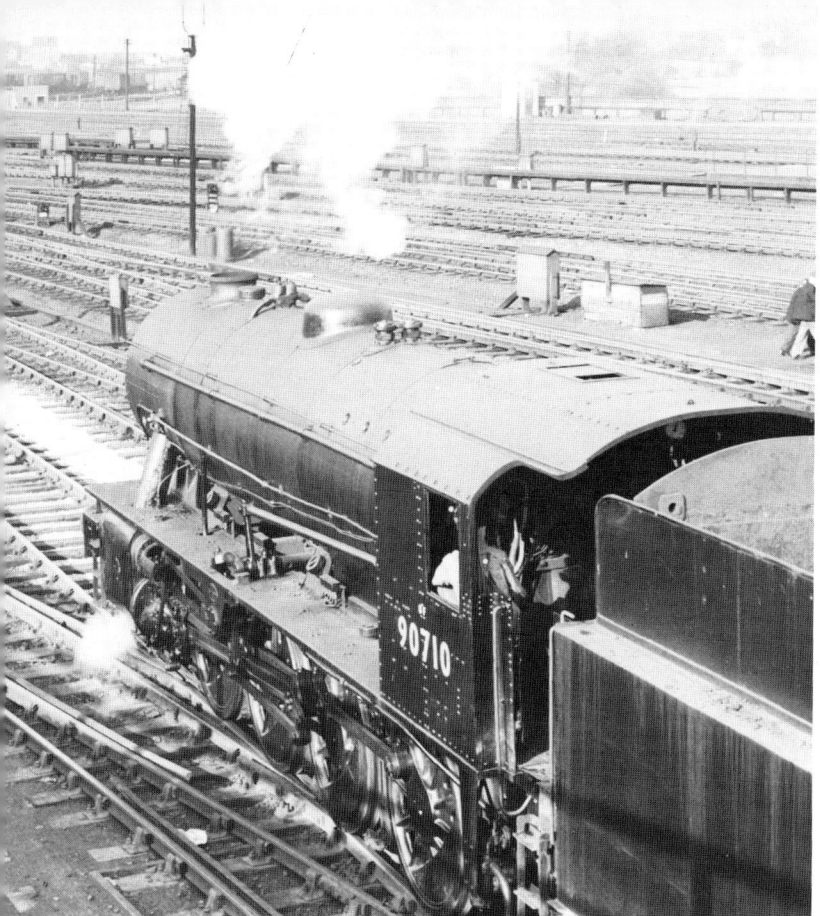

*Left:* In ex-works condition, an Austerity 2-8-0 No 90710 is seen steaming along one of the Chester goods lines at Crewe on 19 September 1957. These engines were reputed to be very rough riders and were rarely if ever used on passenger trains.

*Below:* In ex-works condition and possibly running in after an overall at Crewe Works, BR Standard 2-10-0 No 92060 is seen passing Chester General station on the down through line with a goods train on 5 October 1963. Yellow painted axle box covers on the tender indicate that it is fitted with Timken roller bearings.

*Right:* On 7 August 1958 an ex-LNWR 'Super D' 0-8-0 No 49229 hauls a BR Standard 2-10-0 No 92138 which appeared to be not in steam along the Chester goods lines outside Crewe station en route from the works to the south engine shed. A Fowler 0-6-0 Class 4F can be seen stopped at the signal on the down goods line.

*Below right:* The BR Standard 2-10-0s were a class of engine which survived until the end of steam. In typical late BR finish, No 92085 is pictured leaving the goods yard by Chester General station with a goods train bound for Wrexham on a summer's evening in 1966.

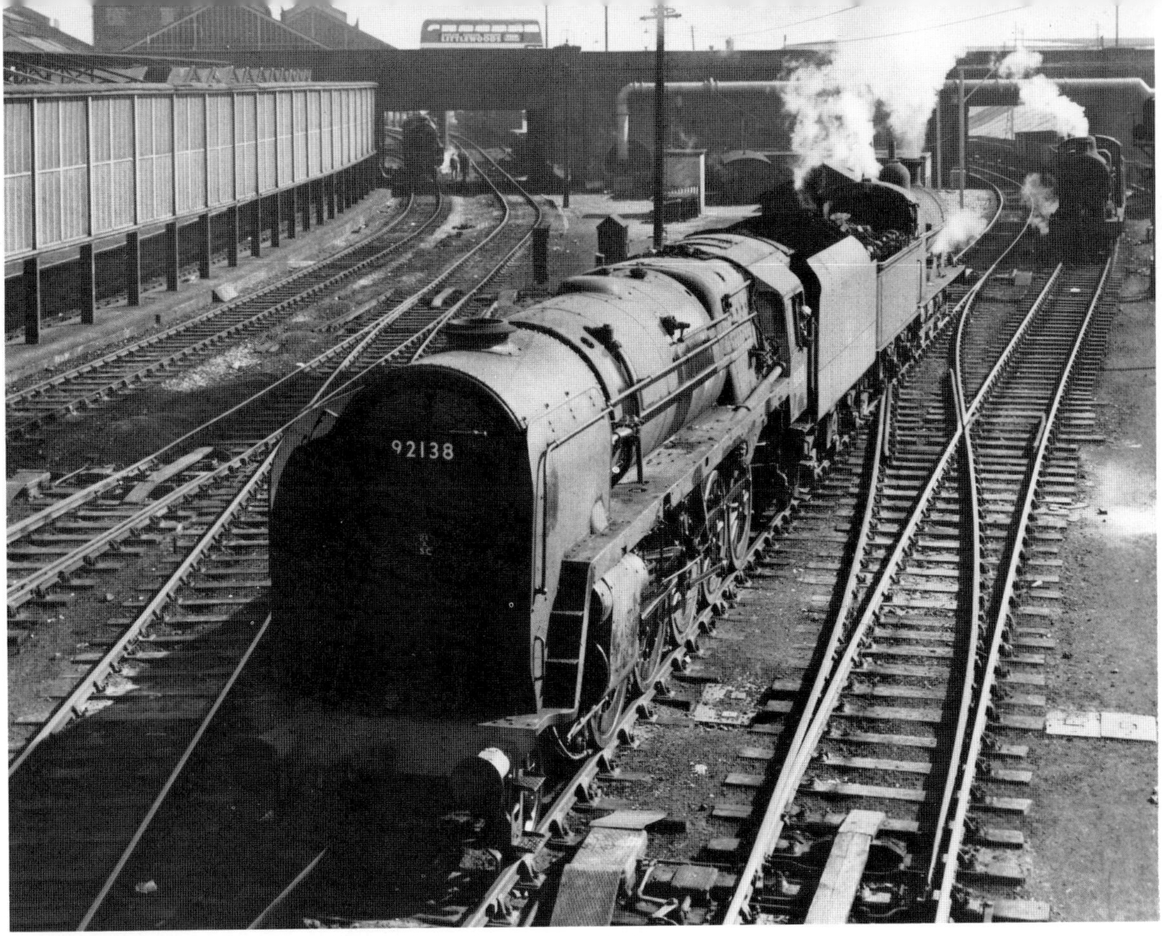
92138

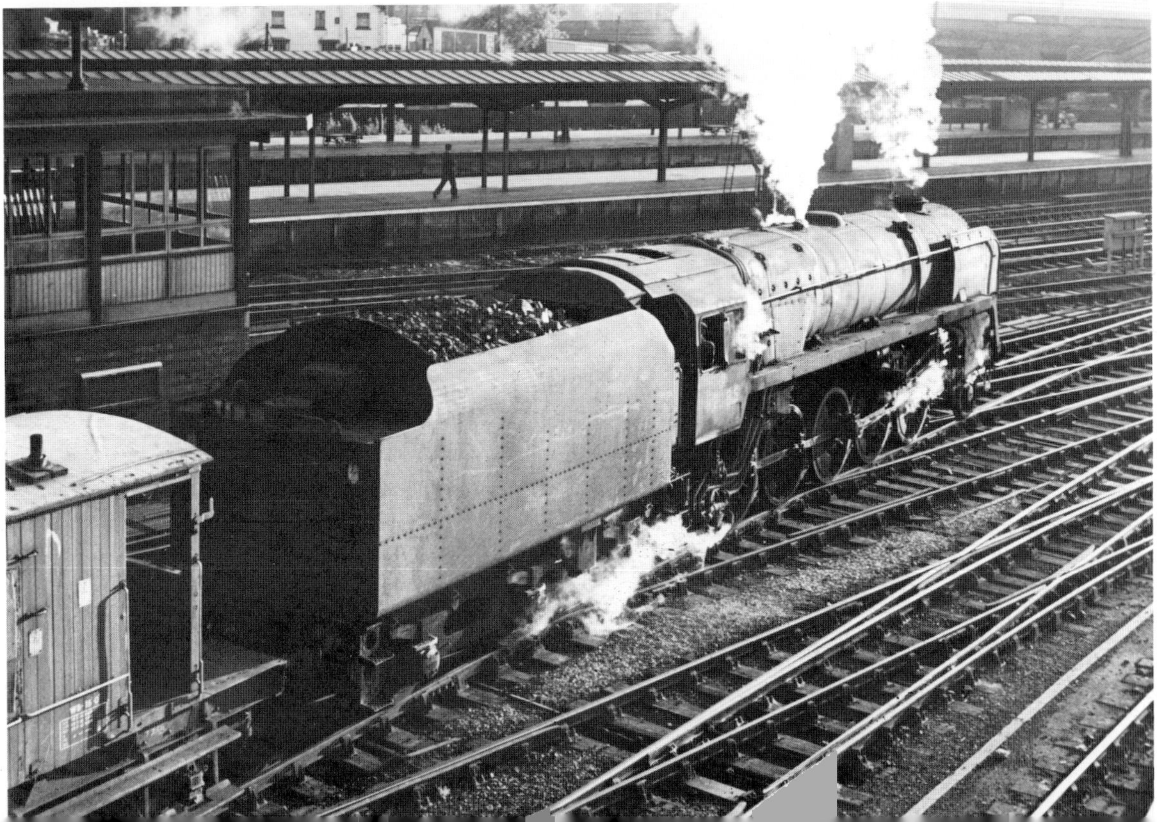

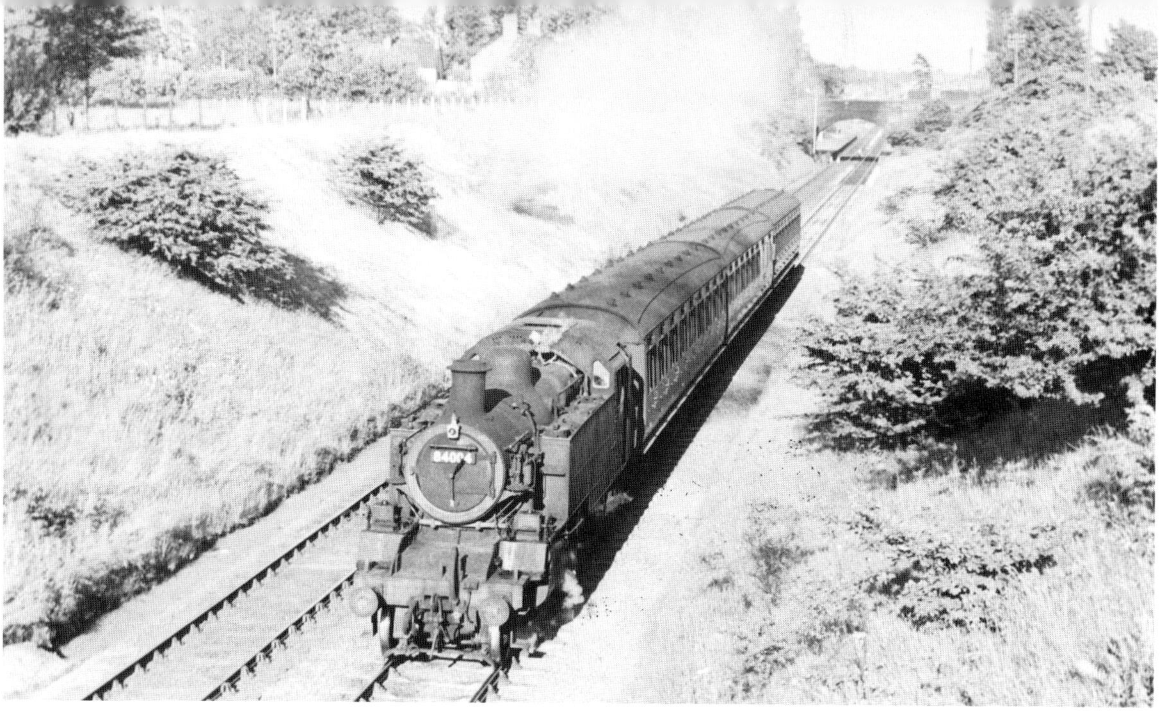

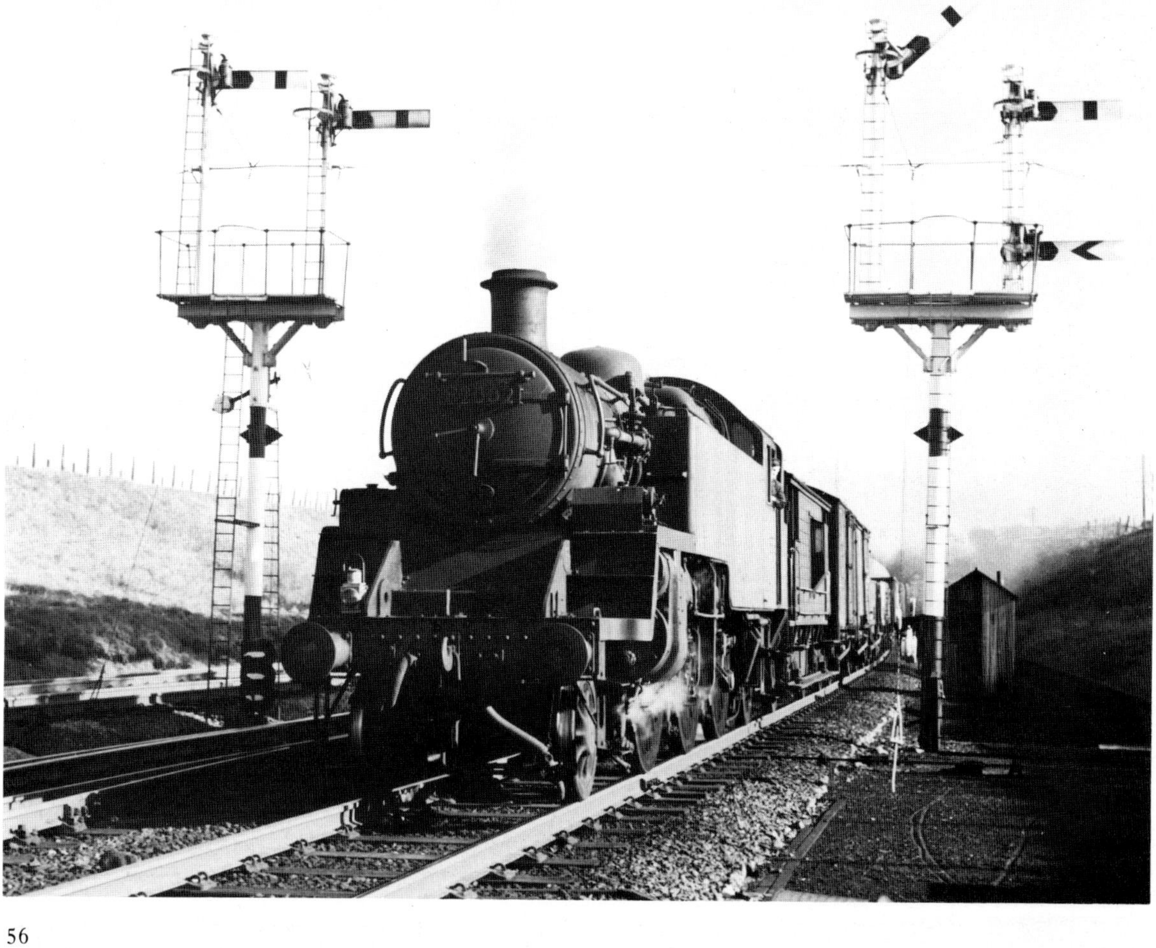

*Top left:* By the mid-1950s the ex-LNER locomotives working on trains out of Chester Northgate station had been replaced by engines of BR Standard or ex-LMS design. On 9 October 1955 BR Standard Class 2MT 2-6-2T No 84004 is shown leaving Blacon for Sealand with the 19.00 train from Chester Northgate to Shotton (High Level).

*Left:* On 27 February 1960 a BR Standard 2-6-2T No 82002 passes the down bracket signals at Saltney junction with a transfer goods train from Chester to Mold junction yard. By this time this class of engine had replaced the ex-GWR tank engines of similar wheel arrangement at Chester.

*Top:* The WR shed at Chester had a number of BR Standard Class 3 2-6-2T engines on the strength towards the end of its existence. One of these No 82003 is shown at the head of the 15.13 Birkenhead to Ruabon train nearing its next stop at Gresford on 6 August 1959.

*Above:* Towards the end of steam a batch of BR Standard 2-6-0 Class 4s were drafted into the Chester area. Looking in rather run down condition No 76047 waits in Platform 3 at Chester General in the summer of 1967 with a train for Birkenhead Woodside.

*Above:* For a few years after nationalisation, ex-LNER engines could still be seen in and around Chester (Northgate). With a 6D (Northgate) shedplate on the smokebox J10 0-6-0 No 65143 was pictured running on to the turntable at its home shed on 8 September 1954.

*Below:* With the sound of the exhaust carrying two miles across the quiet Cheshire countryside, ex-LMS 4-6-2 No 46243 *City of Lancaster* climbs from Weaver junction to Acton Bridge on 29 August 1959 with the southbound 'Royal Scot' on its non-stop run from Carlisle to London Euston. The train is loaded to its standard complement of 13 coaches and only a grey haze emerges from the chimney which indicates good coal and a good fireman.

*Above:* Ex-LMS 4-6-2 No 46246 *City of Manchester* was one of the last of its class to retain the sloping top smokebox which was a legacy from the days when it ran with a streamlined casing. The engine is shown entering Crewe station from the south with the down 'Mid-Day Scot', the 13.15 London Euston to Glasgow Central express on 19 August 1957.

*Below:* In the late 1950s a new lightweight express appeared in the timetables named the 'Caledonian' and running in both directions between London (Euston) and Glasgow (Central). The train with its standard formation of eight coaches is pictured passing Crewe station on the up through line on 29 July 1958 on its nonstop run from Carlisle to London headed by ex-LMS 4-6-2 No 46239 *City of Chester*.

*Above:* Badly delayed by preceding late running trains ex-LMS 4-6-2 No 46244 *King George VI* drifts down the hill past Acton Bridge signalbox on a July Saturday in 1955 at the head of the northbound 'Royal Scot'. Note the headboard with a tartan background which this train usually carried.

*Below:* The last two ex-LMS 'Duchess' class Pacifics to be built differed from the other members of the class chiefly in the design of the pony truck under the firebox and in the depth of the cabsides. The penultimate member of the class No 46256 *Sir William A. Stanier FRS* is pictured passing Crewe on a June Saturday in 1957 at the head of the down 'Red Rose' express from London (Euston) to Liverpool (Lime Street).

*Above right:* Ex-LMS 4-6-2 No 46242 *City of Glasgow* was one of the engines involved in the disastrous Harrow smash in 1952 afterwards being rebuilt identical to the earlier non-streamlined engines with solid framing in front of the cylinders. The engine was photographed on a summer Saturday in 1955 north of Hartford on the West Coast main line at the head of the down 'Lakes Express' from London (Euston) to Windermere.

*Right:* At the end of 1957 it was decided to paint some of the ex-LMS Pacifics maroon colour with yellow lining out in the LMS style and straw coloured numerals on the cabside. One of the 16 'Duchess' class engines so treated No 46248 *City of Leeds* was pictured in the new roundhouse at Crewe north shed on 26 February 1961.

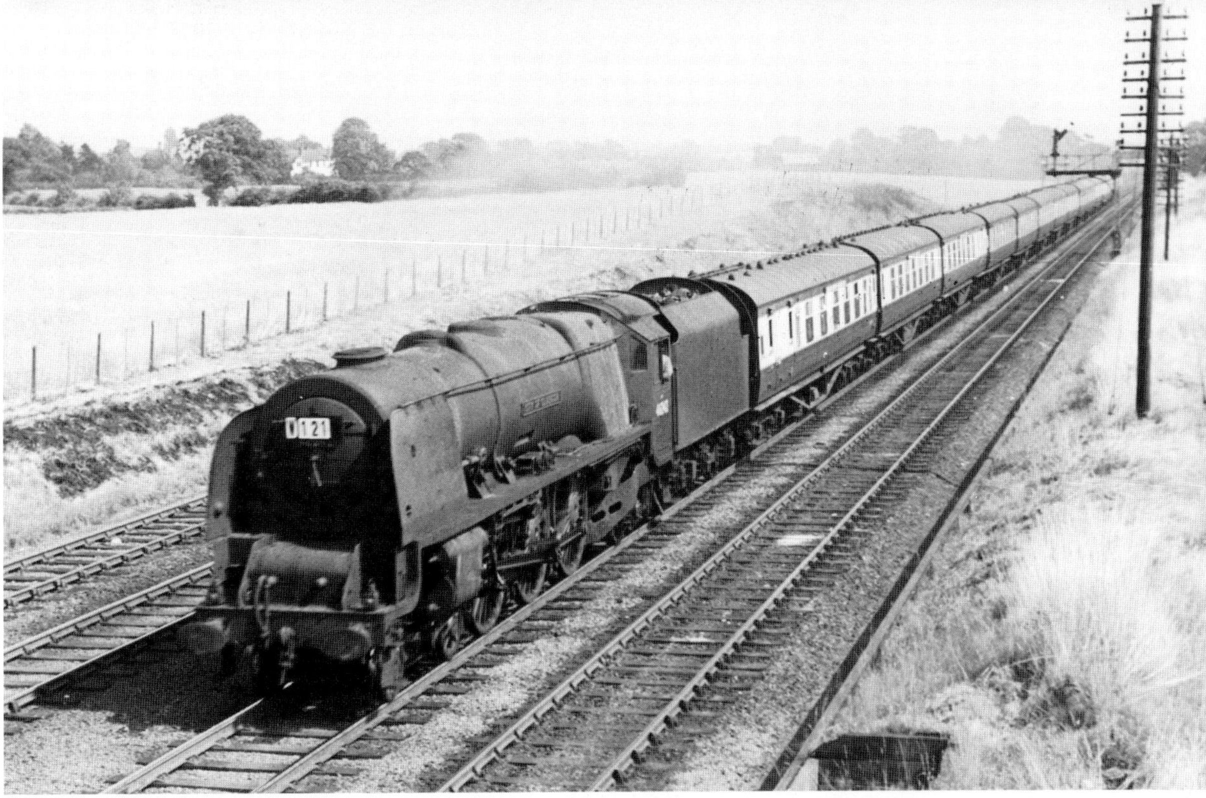

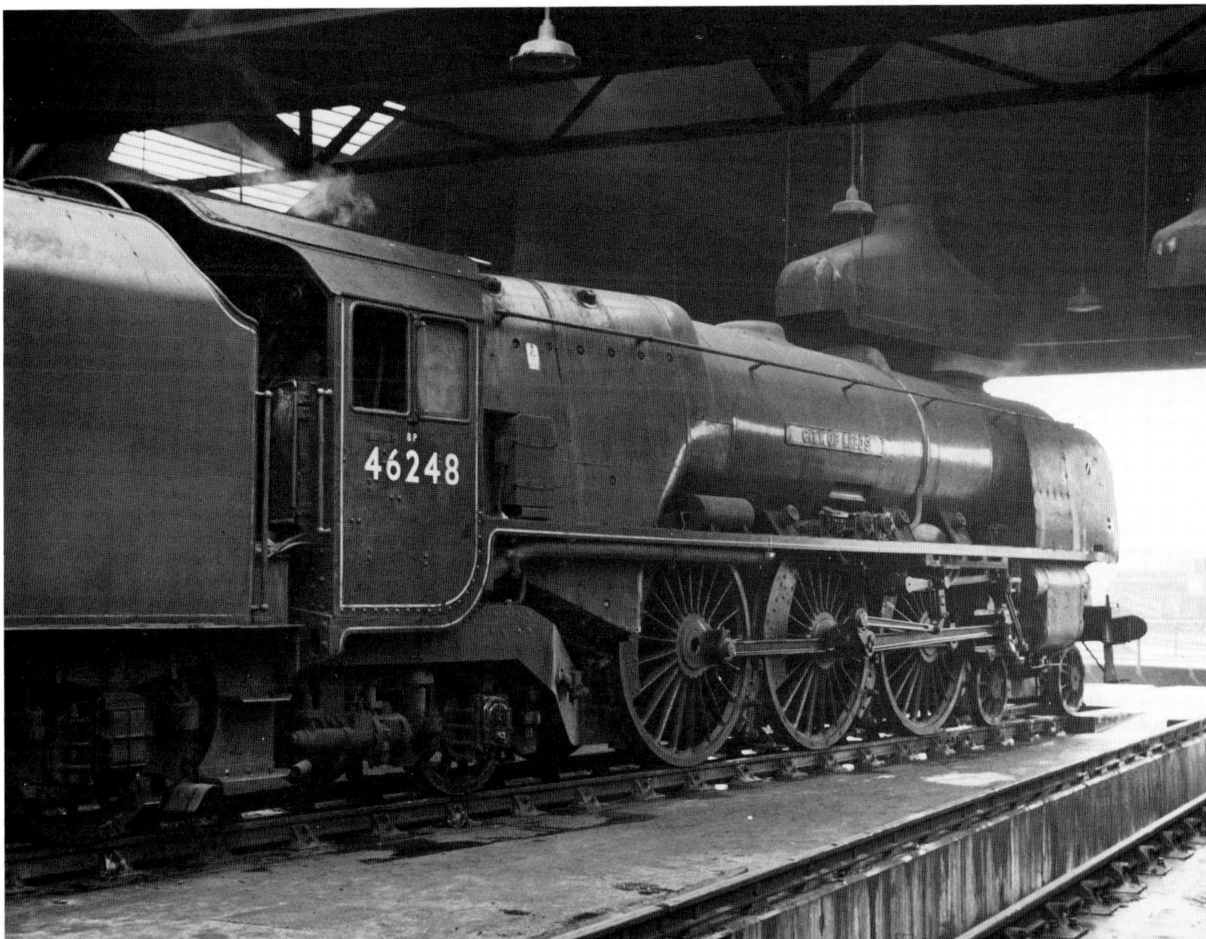
46248
CITY OF LEEDS

*Above:* As diesel and electric locomotives came to be used on the West Coast main line the ex-LMS Pacifics saw more use on the line from Crewe to Holyhead.
No 46240 *City of Coventry* is shown running into Chester General station on 5 March 1961 at the head of the up 'Emerald Isle' express. The 12.45 (Sundays) Holyhead to London (Euston).

*Left:* Having been diverted to the slow line at Mold junction ex-LMS 4-6-2 No 46233 *Duchess of Sutherland* heads towards Chester on 20 April 1960 with the 08.10 train from Holyhead to Crewe. Seeing that the train consists of six coaches only it hardly seems to warrant the use of a locomotive this size.

*Above:* With a cold east wind blowing the exhaust across the train, ex-LMS 4-6-2 No 46204 *Princess Louise* runs southwards through Crewe station towards its first stop at Rugby early in 1951 with the 14.10 express from Liverpool (Lime St) to London (Euston).

*Right:* On Sunday 22 July 1962 4-6-2 No 46200 *The Princess Royal* waits at Chester General station with a special train for the Railway Correspondence & Travel Society bound for Holyhead. On the left stands the old No 3A signalbox looking as though it has not had its windows cleaned for some considerable time.

*Above:* An ex-LMS rebuilt 'Royal Scot' No 46159 *The Royal Air Force* sets off from Chester on 2 June 1962 with the 14.30 relief express to London (Euston). In the background a 'Duchess' class engine waits to take over the main train from Bangor, due to depart for London 10 minutes later.

*Below:* As ex-LMS rebuilt 'Royal Scot' No 46156 *The South Wales Borderer* runs into Chester General station on 23 June 1962 with an afternoon relief train from Crewe to Llandudno, the fireman looks out and sees signs of modernisation in the shape of an English Electric Type 4 diesel-electric locomotive standing on the up through line.

*Above:* On a summer Saturday afternoon in 1954, rebuilt 'Royal Scot' No 46167 *Civil Service Rifleman* leans to the curve past Waverton station as it heads towards Crewe with the southbound 'Welshman' on its nonstop run from Chester to London (Euston). The train includes through coaches from Portmadoc and Pwllheli to London in addition to the main part from Bangor.

*Below:* Prior to the Pacifics being displaced on the West Coast main line, the 09.20 express from Crewe to Holyhead was usually hauled by a Crewe North based engine of Class 6 or 7. With steam to spare, rebuilt 'Royal Scot' No 46128 *The Lovat Scouts* was pictured on 10 March 1956 heading out from Chester with this train towards its next stop at Prestatyn.

*Above:* Still painted in its last LMS passenger livery of black lined out in maroon and straw but carrying a BR number, parallel boiler 'Royal Scot' No 46110 *Grenadier Guardsman* is shown passing Crewe station in 1951 with an express from London (Euston) to Liverpool (Lime Street). The station entrance is visible above the third coach on the Nantwich road bridge.

*Below:* Diverted because of engineering work in progress ahead at Saltney, rebuilt 'Royal Scot' No 46136 *The Border Regiment* is shown running from the up fast to the up slow line at Mold junction at the head of a Bangor to London (Euston) express on a Sunday afternoon in 1954. The two lines on the left form the start of the branch to Mold and Denbigh. The island platform which is Saltney Ferry station is to be seen between them just beyond the bridge and also beyond the bridge on the left is Mold junction motive power depot.

*Right:* Loaded to 15 coaches and with both name and number invisible beneath the grime, an ex-LMS rebuilt 'Patriot' 4-6-0 crosses the River Dee bridge at Chester with the 11.15 London (Euston) to Bangor Express in the summer of 1951.

*Below:* On a very busy July Saturday afternoon in 1955, ex-LMS Compound 4-4-0 No 40936 passes through Acton Bridge station en route from Warrington to Crewe with a through train from Blackpool to Birmingham (New St).

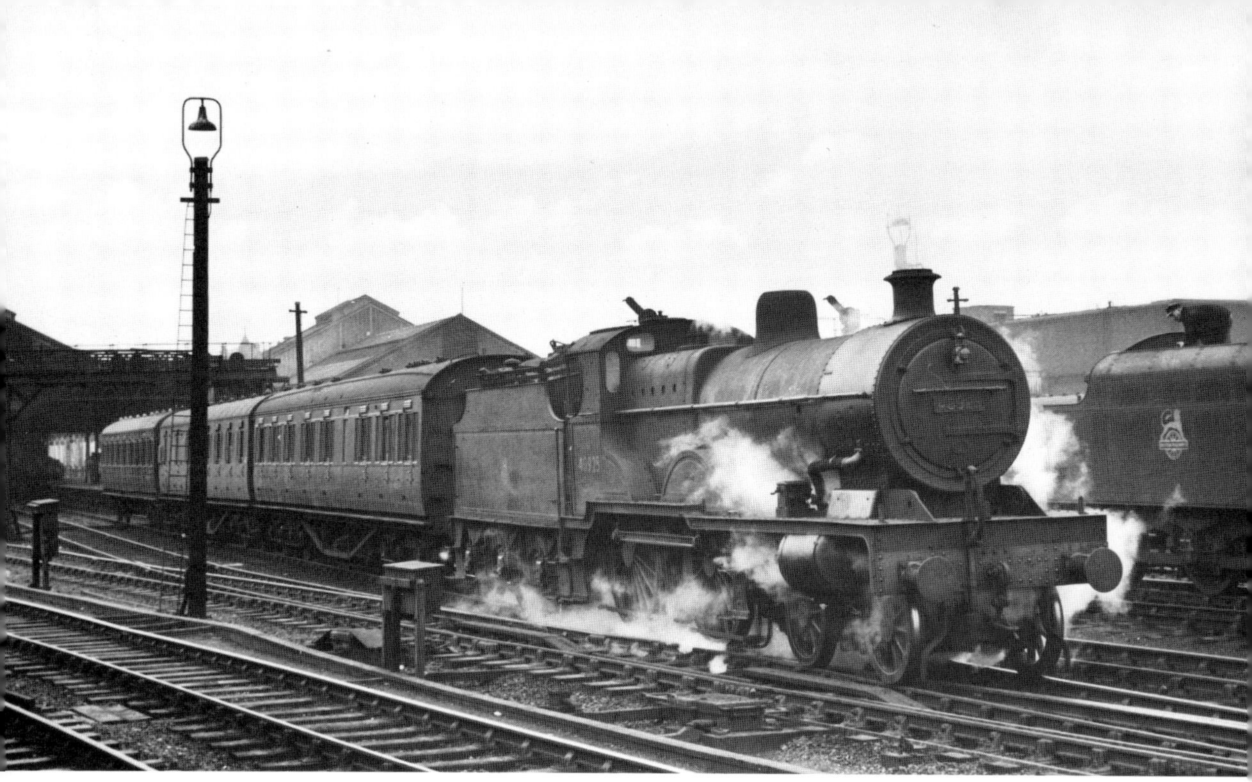

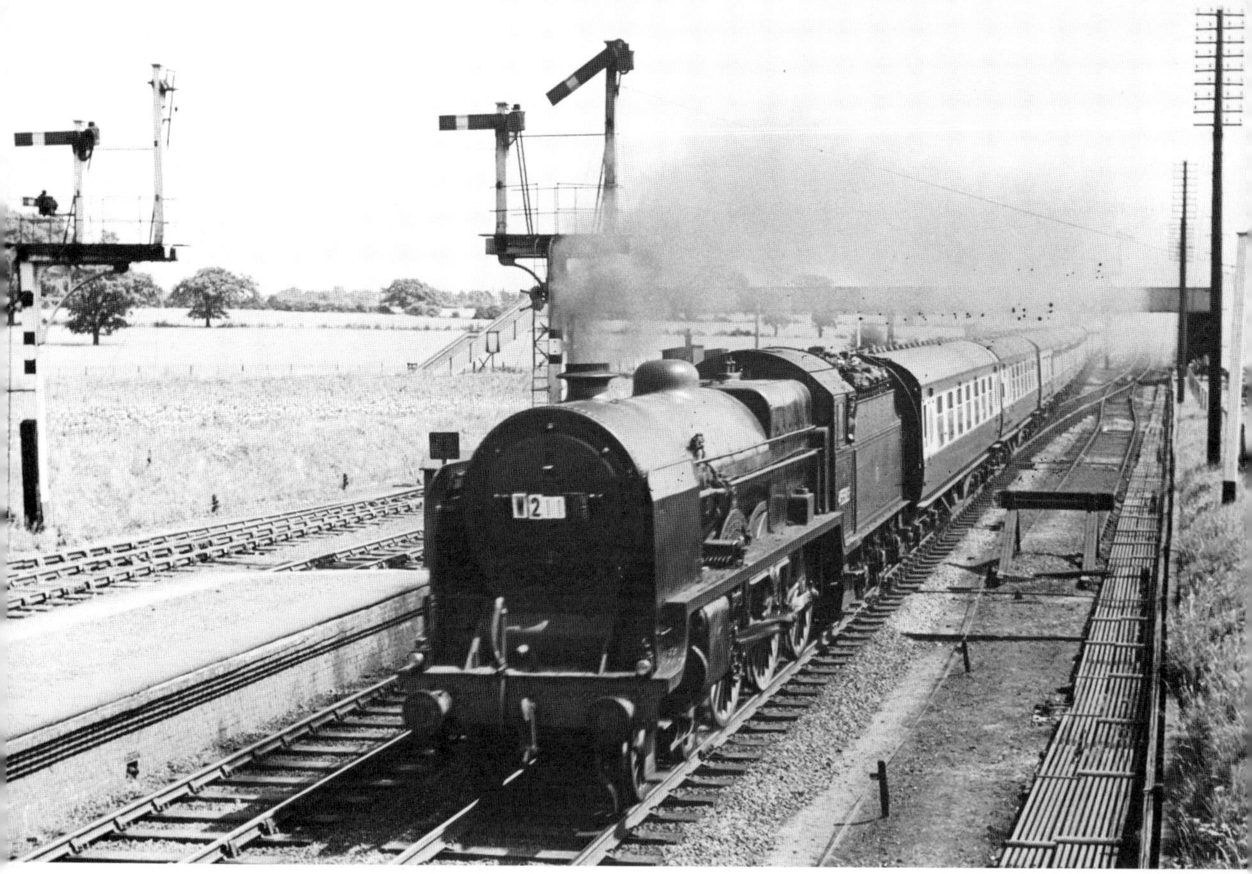

*Above left:* On 17 August 1957 ex-LMS Compound 4-4-0 No 40925 sets off from Crewe with the 15.25 stopping train to Shrewsbury via Whitchurch. Judging from the steam to be seen coming from beneath the boiler, the engine would not seem to be in the best of condition.

*Left:* On the downhill stretch of line from Hartford to Weaver junction some pretty high speeds could be achieved by northbound expresses. Running late and sounding as though it was making up time, ex-LMS 'Patriot' 4-6-0 No 45503 *The Royal Leicestershire Regiment* passes Acton Bridge station with a down express on a July Saturday afternoon in 1955.

*Above:* Although classed as express passenger engines, the ex-LMS 'Patriot' 4-6-0s could be often seen working fitted freight trains. No 45533 *Lord Rathmore* was photographed performing such a task running northwards towards Dutton Viaduct and Weaver junction on 23 May 1959.

*Right:* Heavily loaded with a Cunard ocean liner special, an Edge Hill ex-LMS 'Jubilee' 4-6-0 No 45630 *Swaziland* hammers its way up the gradient from Weaver junction in May 1955 on its non-stop run from Liverpool (Riverside) to London (Euston).

*Above:* In mid 1954 rebuilt 'Royal Scot' No 46106 *Gordon Highlander* was fitted with BR type smoke deflectors in place of the normal type carried by the remainder of the class. The engine is pictured in its later guise leaving Crewe on a June Saturday in 1957 with the 12.50 express from Bangor to London (Euston).

*Below:* Rebuilt in 1935 from the experimental high pressure compound locomotive No 6399 *Fury*, taper boilered 'Royal Scot' No 46170 *British Legion* was always unique in having a Stanier cab, differently shaped outside steam pipes and a boiler which would not fit any other member of the class. The engine is pictured just north of Acton Bridge station on 23 May 1959 at the head of the 10.40 express from London (Euston) to Blackpool (Central).

*Above:* Judging by the clouds of smoke coming from the chimney of ex-LMS 4-6-2 No 46209 *Princess Beatrice*, the state of the fire is not all that it should be. Despite this the engine was going well and was right on time as it headed north towards Weaver junction on 7 August 1957 with the down 'Mid-Day Scot'.

*Below:* Normally, the engine which started the journey from Bangor with the 12.30 express to London was replaced at Chester by a larger one for the remainder of the run, the replacement loco having worked down from Crewe earlier in the day. About to start the second leg, ex-LMS 4-6-2 No 46203 *Princess Margaret Rose* is shown standing at the head of the train at Chester General on 7 August 1961.

*Above:* On 2 August 1957 ex-LMS 4-6-2 No 46210 *Lady Patricia* and 'Patriot' 4-6-0 No 45550 make light work of the climb from Weaver junction to Acton Bridge with the 'Manxman'. The 14.10 express from Liverpool (Lime St) to London (Euston). Seeing that the train's first stop is at Rugby, it is very likely that the pilot engine will be working right through to London.

*Below:* Many different types of engine could be found acting as pilot at the north end of Crewe station. On a June Saturday in 1957, ex-LMS 'Patriot' 4-6-0 No 45546 *Fleetwood* was to be seen shunting an odd assortment of ex-LMS vans into the stock sidings adjacent to the Manchester lines.

*Above:* At one time it was intended to rebuild all the ex-LMS 'Patriot' 4-6-0s with the same taper boiler as the converted 'Royal Scots' but in the event only 18 of the 52 members of the class were so modified. One of these No 45514 *Holyhead* is shown between Tattenhall junction and Waverton on 8 September 1954 at the head of the down 'Welshman', the 11.15 from London (Euston) to Bangor, Portmadoc and Pwllheli.

*Right:* In the early 1960s ex-LMS 'Jubilee' class engines started to appear on the Paddington to Birkenhead expresses between Shrewsbury and Chester. Following the introduction of diesel haulage between Shrewsbury and London, one of these No 45577 *Bengal* is shown setting off from Chester General station on 9 August 1963 with the 16.30 Birkenhead to Paddington express.

*Right:* The ex-LMS 'Jubilee' class engines shedded at Blackpool had regular workings to and from London (Euston). On 26 May 1958 No 45584 *North West Frontier* was photographed north of Hartford heading homewards with the 13.35 express from Euston to Blackpool (Central).

*Below right:* The engines which were used for shunting in Crewe locomotive works were many and varied and included small tender types as well as tanks. On Sunday 22 November 1959 the complement included ex-L&YR 3F 0-6-0 No 52464 with a round topped firebox pictured standing next to a similar engine with a firebox of the Belpaire type.

*Below:* Having passed through the short tunnel under the northern part of the city and crossed the Shropshire Union Canal, ex-LMS 'Jubilee' class 4-6-0 No 45618 *New Hebrides* cuts across the corner of the city walls by the water tower at Chester on 13 August 1961 with the 14.20 stopping train from Chester General station to Llandudno. It is a Sunday afternoon and the man at the lineside is acting as look out for a track gang higher up the line.

*Above:* Running through a smoke haze laid by the train seen travelling in the opposite direction, ex-LMS 'Jubilee' 4-6-0 No 45686 *St Vincent* approaches Tattenhall junction between Chester and Crewe with an express goods train from Holyhead to London (Broad St) on 8 September 1954.

*Below:* Some of the ex-LMS 'Jubilee' 4-6-0s were fitted with the Fowler 3,500gal water capacity tenders. One of these No 45603 *Solomon Islands* is seen between Waverton and Chester on 19 September 1955 with an afternoon express from Crewe to Holyhead.

*Above:* In 1932 Messrs Kitsons Ltd, designed and built five 0-4-0STs for the LMS Railway. In 1953 a further five engines, similar but with reshaped tanks and increased bunker space, were built at the Horwich Works of British Rail, one of these later engines No 47007 is shown shunting near to Shore Road in Birkenhead docks on an August day in 1955.

*Below:* A Sunday morning tour of Crewe locomotive works could usually be guaranteed to produce a rare subject or two for the camera and 22 November 1959 was no exception. Pictured standing in the paintshop yard on that day is an ex-LNWR saddle tank which had been withdrawn from departmental use and an ex-LNWR coal tank No 58926 which had been purchased for private preservation and is at the time of writing still in existence.

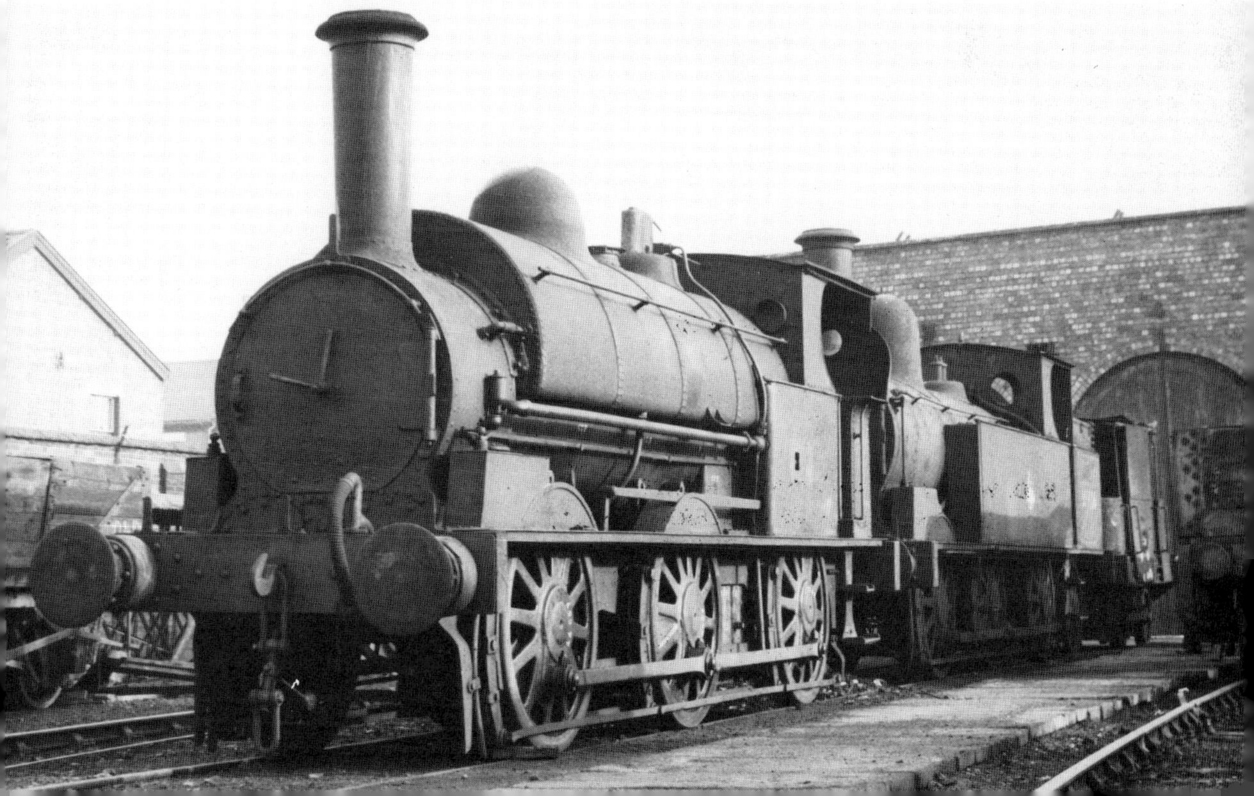

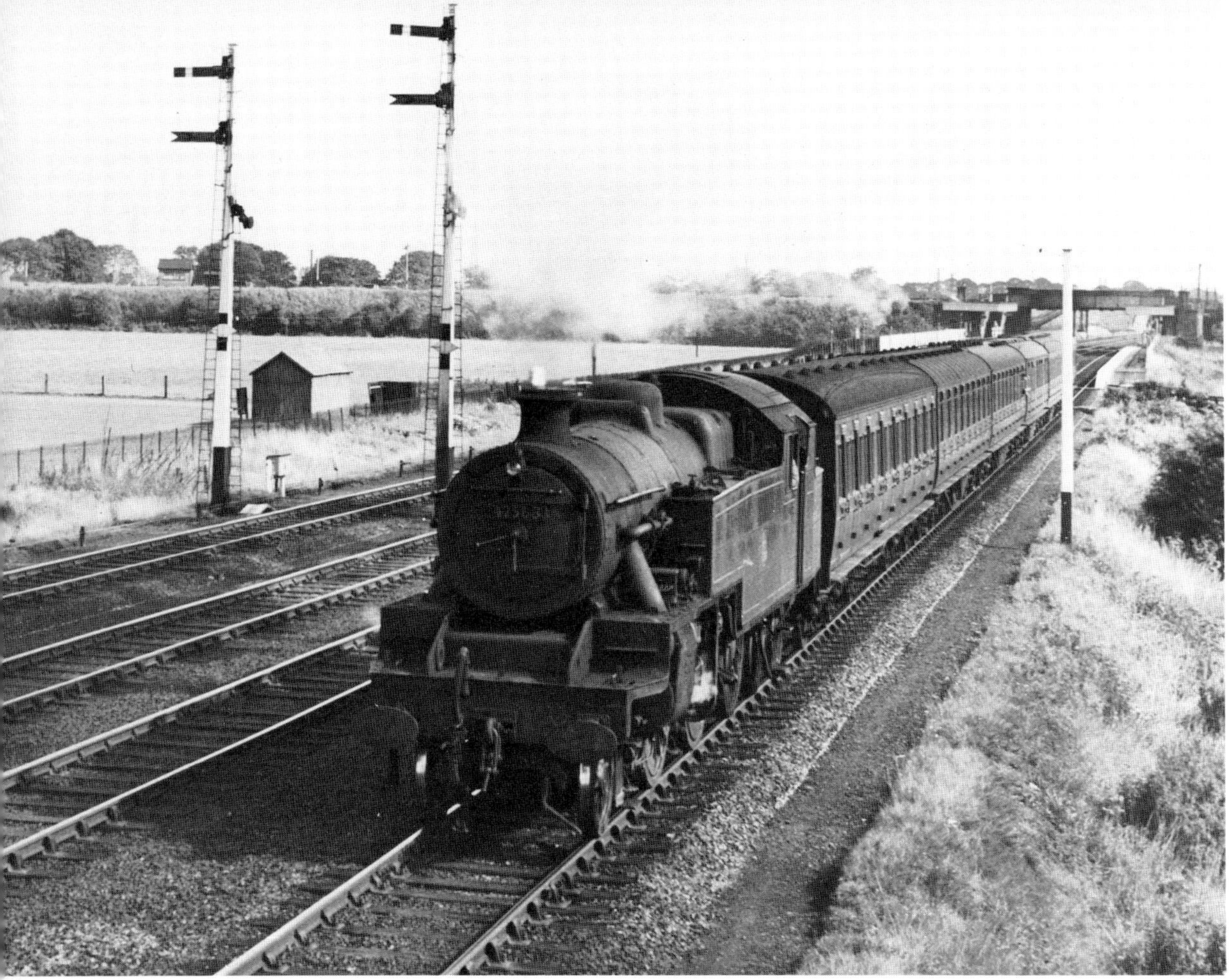

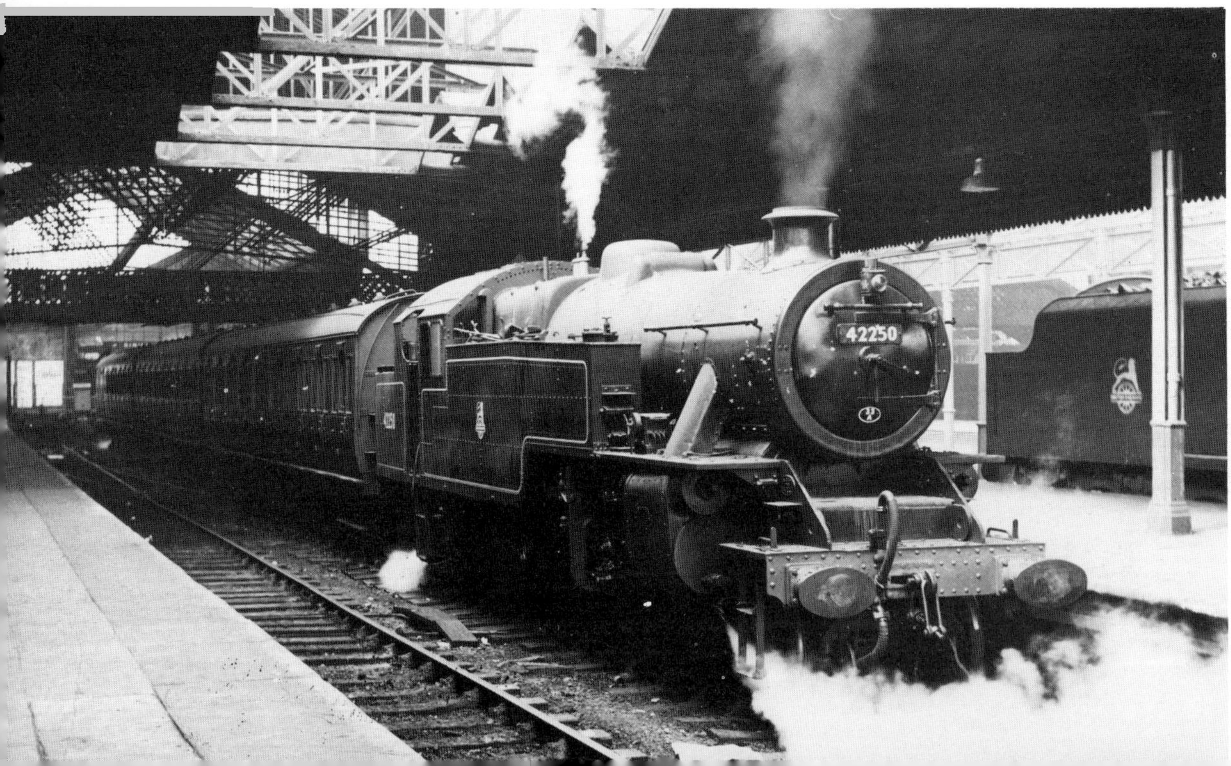
42250

*Left:* On an August afternoon in 1954, Stanier 2-6-4T No 42568 is shown setting off from Shotton (Low Level) with a stopping train from Chester to Rhyl. The line on the embankment in the background is the ex-LNER one from Wrexham (Central) to Seacombe.

*Below left:* With a 33A (Plaistow) shedplate on the smokebox door, Fairburn 2-6-4T No 42250 is a long way from its home shed as it stands in No 4 bay at Crewe station on an afternoon in 1953 with a stopping train to Shrewsbury. From the engine's condition, it is very likely that it is running in after an overhaul at the works at Crewe.

*Right:* Stanier 2-6-4T No 42443 approaches Chester with the 09.30 train from Birkenhead (Woodside) to Bournemouth (West) on 30 April 1960. This engine will only work the train to Chester where a Western Region tender engine will couple on to the other end to work the train as far as Oxford.

*Below:* Chester Northgate station on 18 May 1959 and Fowler 2-6-4T No 42393 waits to depart with the 12.42 train to Manchester Central. This station was the Chester terminus of the Cheshire Lines Committee and also the terminus of the ex-LNER services to Shotton (High Level) and Wrexham (Central).

*Left:* The last 30 Fowler 2-6-4Ts were provided with side window cabs and doors similar to the Stanier versions. One of these No 42421 is shown approaching Crewe station from the south on 28 March 1959 with a train of empty stock. Signs of the forthcoming electrification are very apparent.

*Centre left:* In the middle of 1966 a rather decrepit looking 'Jinty', ex-LMS 0-6-0T, No 47324 shunts a train of vans on the down centre through line at Chester (General). On the right a BR Standard Class 5 4-6-0 No 73159 stands in Platform 4 with a down North Wales express.

*Bottom left:* Despite its express passenger headcode ex-LMS 'Jinty' 0-6-0T No 47680 is actually hauling a stores train of some kind as it heads towards Crewe station from the south on 19 August 1957, bound for the locomotive works by the North junction.

*Below:* Stanier 2-6-2T No 40106 is seen leaving Blacon on 6 June 1960 with the 14.05 train from Chester (Northgate) to Wrexham (Central). The crew seem to have left a large can of oil on the engine's platform in front of the outside steam pipe.

*Bottom:* On a very wintry day in 1955, Ivatt ex-LMS 2-6-2T No 41244 crosses over from the down fast to the down slow line at Saltney junction with the 10.25 train from Chester (General) to Denbigh via the Mold branch, it was not usual for this train to include a horsebox as shown.

*Above:* Some of the Ivatt ex-LMS 2-6-2T engines were fitted with equipment for working auto trains and one of these No 41276 is shown heading towards Mold junction on 28 May 1958 with the 10.30 stopping train from Chester to Rhyl.

*Below:* The ex-LNWR 0-8-0 'Super Ds' were active in the Chester area almost to the end of their existence. No 49081 was pictured heading away from the city on the down fast line bound for Mold junction with a loose coupled goods train on 25 May 1957.

*Above right:* The ex-LNWR 0-8-0s of Class G2a were known amongst enginemen as 'Super Ds'. One of these No 49355 is shown making rather heavy going of the climb from Weaver junction towards Acton Bridge with a very mixed collection of rolling stock on 31 July 1956.

*Right:* The ex-LMS Class 2MT Ivatt 2-6-0s were used to replace some of the older Great Western engines in the mid-Wales area in the late 1950s. One member of the class No 46513 is shown making a very vigorous start from Oswestry with the 19.25 train to Whitchurch on 26 July 1960.

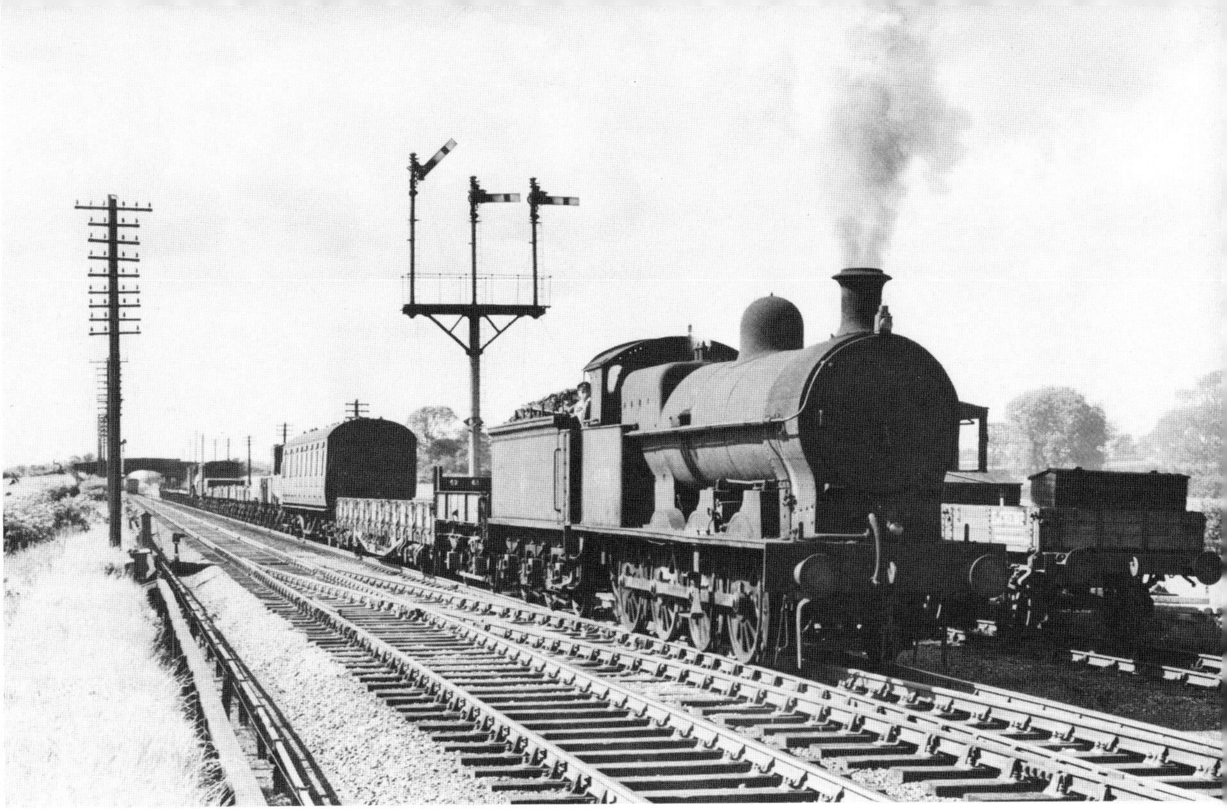

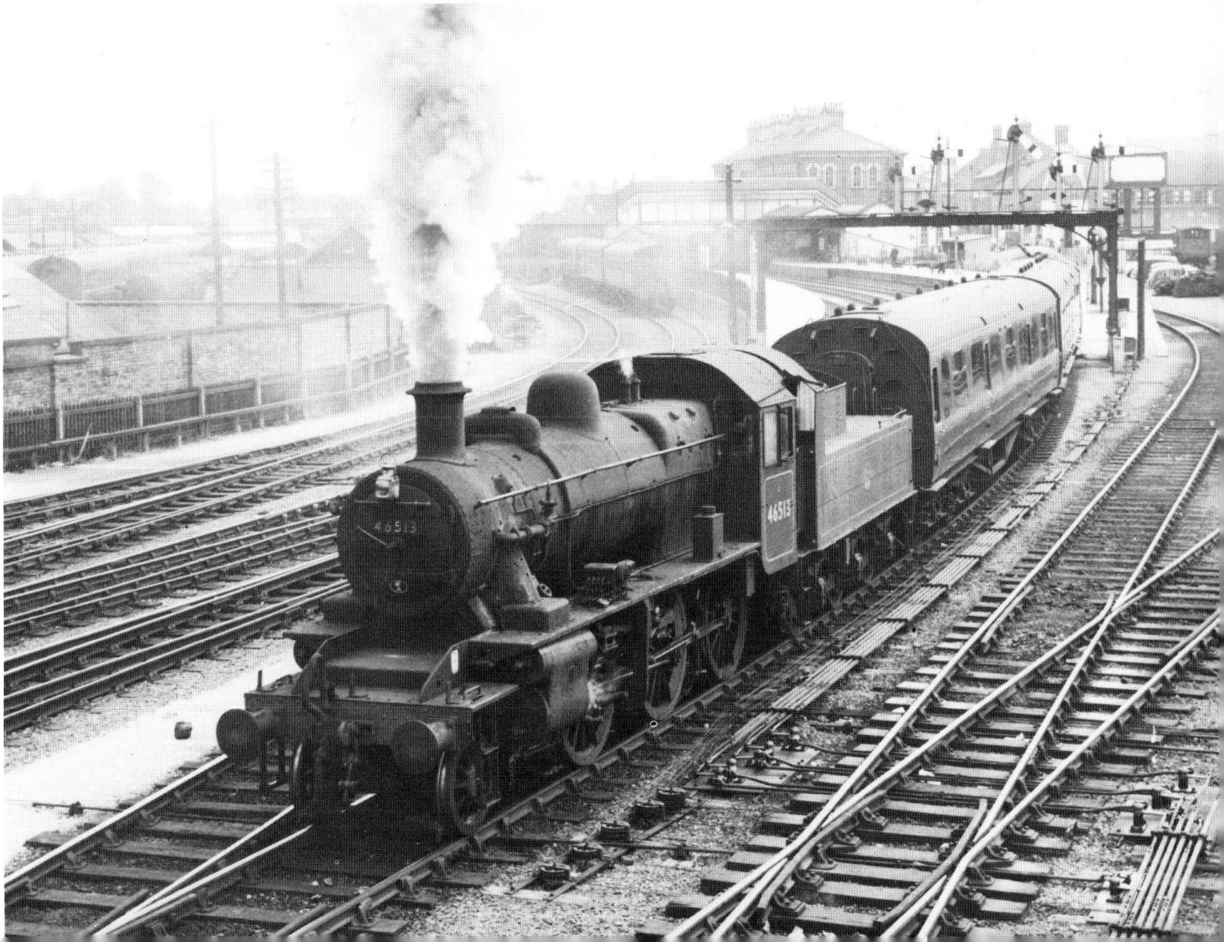
46513
46513

*Left:* With their tender cabs the ex-LMS Ivatt 2-6-0s were quite comfortable engines to work on when used in reverse. Deputising for the usual ex-GW auto train No 46516 coupled to a 'B' set is seen nearing Oswestry on 26 July 1960 with the 15.10 train from Gobowen.

*Centre left:* With the provision of subway lines at Crewe for goods traffic to and from the Manchester and Warrington direction, only goods trains from the Chester line needed to pass across the North junction. On a spring Saturday in 1953 a Fowler Class 4F 0-6-0 No 44359 gums things up a bit as it trundles off the Chester line with a southbound train of empty coal wagons.

*Bottom left:* On 25 May 1957 a Fowler Class 4F 0-6-0 No 44373 ambles along the up fast line from Mold junction towards Chester with a loose coupled goods train. Despite its imposing appearance the overbridge only carried a footpath across the cutting to the adjacent golf course. It did however provide an excellent vantage point for photographers.

*Below:* The ex-LMS compound 4-4-0s were always a familiar sight on the North Wales coast main line until their final demise. One of the class No 41153 is shown passing Shotton (Low Level) in the summer of 1954 at the head of the 13.35 express from Manchester (Exchange) to Holyhead.

*Bottom:* On a summer afternoon in 1952 an ex-LMS compound 4-4-0 No 41120 is pictured between Chester and Waverton with an express from Llandudno to Birmingham (New St). The engine must be steaming well, blowing off at the safety valves as it tackles a rising gradient with a nine coach load.

*Above:* Photographed making the climb from Weaver junction to Acton Bridge at a very rapid pace on a July Saturday in 1956 are ex-Midland Railway Class 2P 4-4-0 No 40396 piloting an unknown 'Jubilee' class 4-6-0 at the head of a southbound express. The crew of the pilot engine must be experiencing one of the customary rough rides that this class of engine gave at high speed as the driver can be seen wedged in the cab cut-out holding on to the roof to steady himself.

*Below:* Acting as station pilot at Crewe north end on 7 August 1958, ex-LMS Class 2P 4-4-0 No 40660 performs a nice easy task hauling an ex-LNER four-wheeled passenger brake van loaded with stores from the works to the south shed.

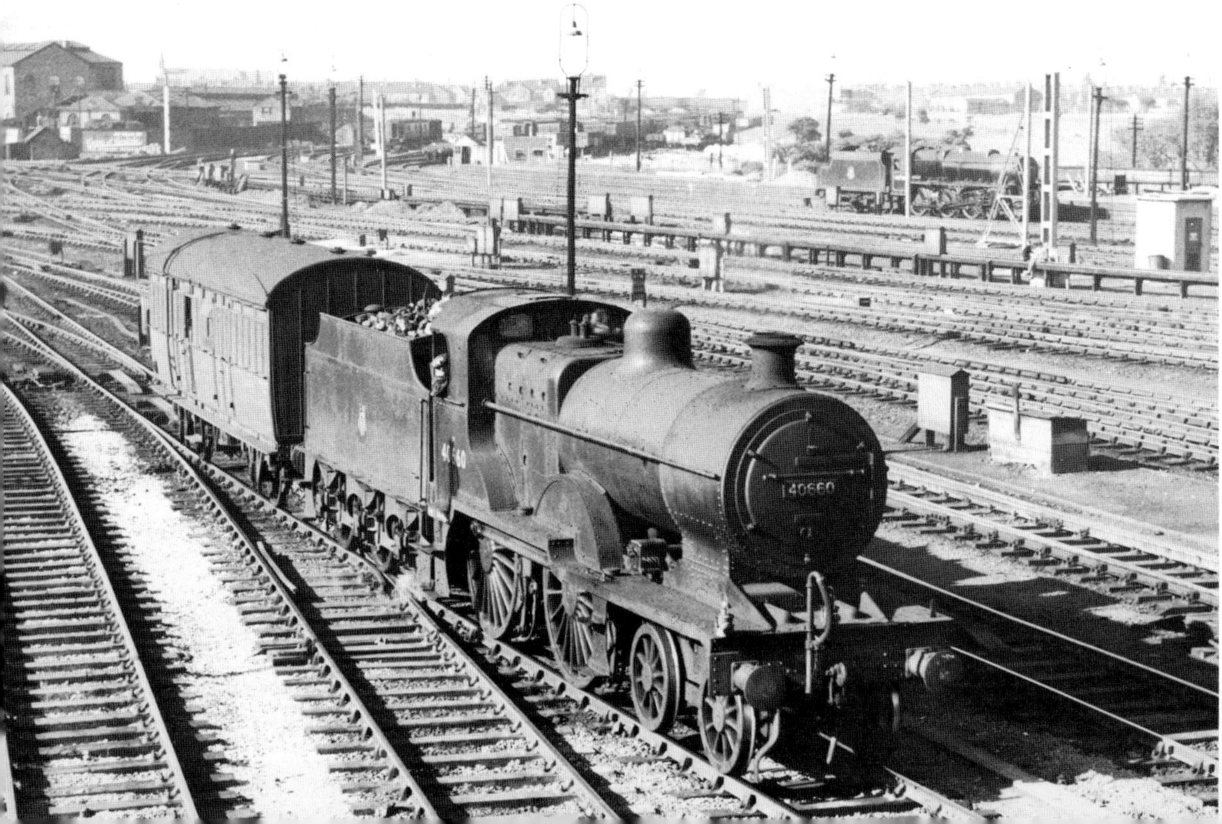

*Above:* On summer Saturdays ex-LMS Fowler Class 5 2-6-0s were regularly to be seen on express passenger work on the north Wales coast main line. One of these engines No 42775 is seen on 15 June 1957 passing Saltney junction at the head of a through train from the Eastern Region bound for Llandudno.

*Below:* Nicknamed 'Crabs' due to the large inclined outside cylinders and high platform at the front end, the ex-LMS Fowler 2-6-0 mixed traffic engines could be found on all types of work. An unusually clean member of the class No 42888 is seen heading a northbound goods train through Acton Bridge station on 2 August 1957.

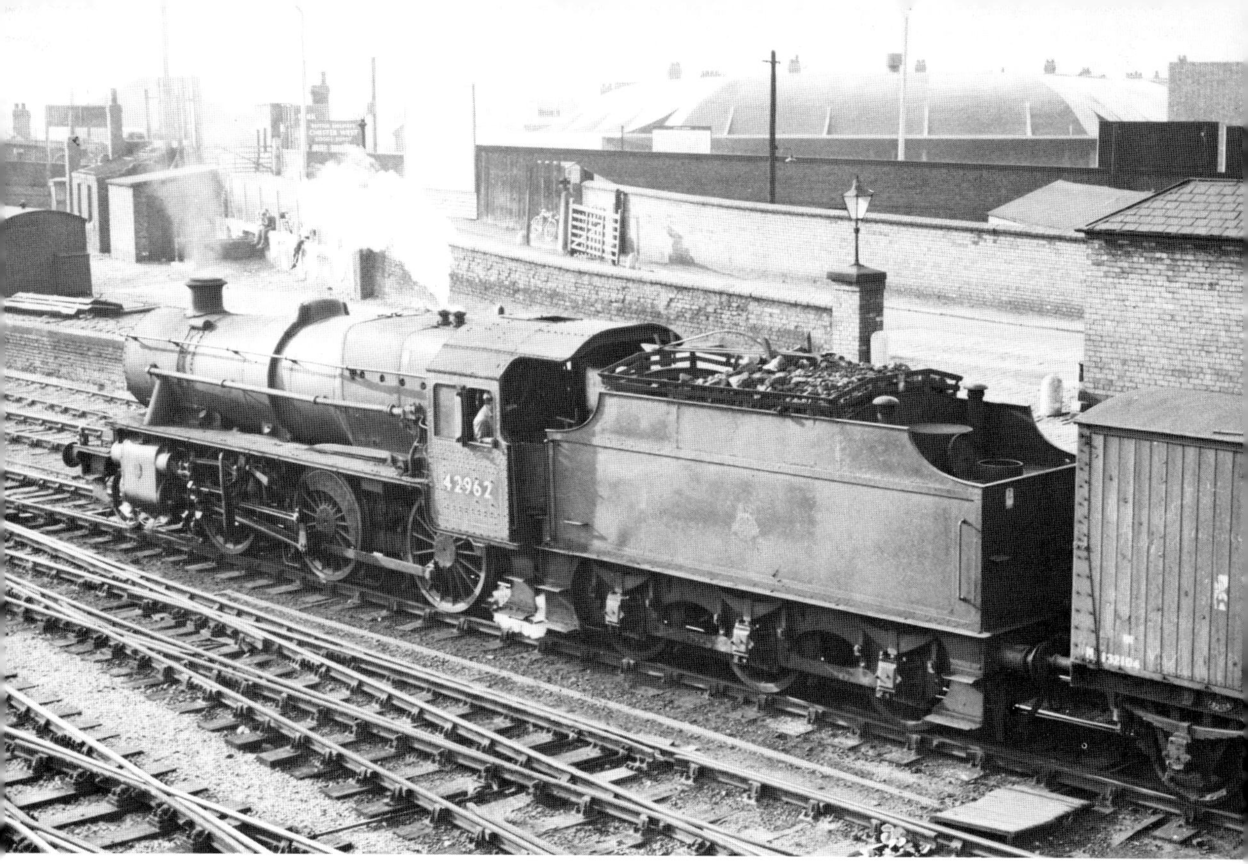
42962

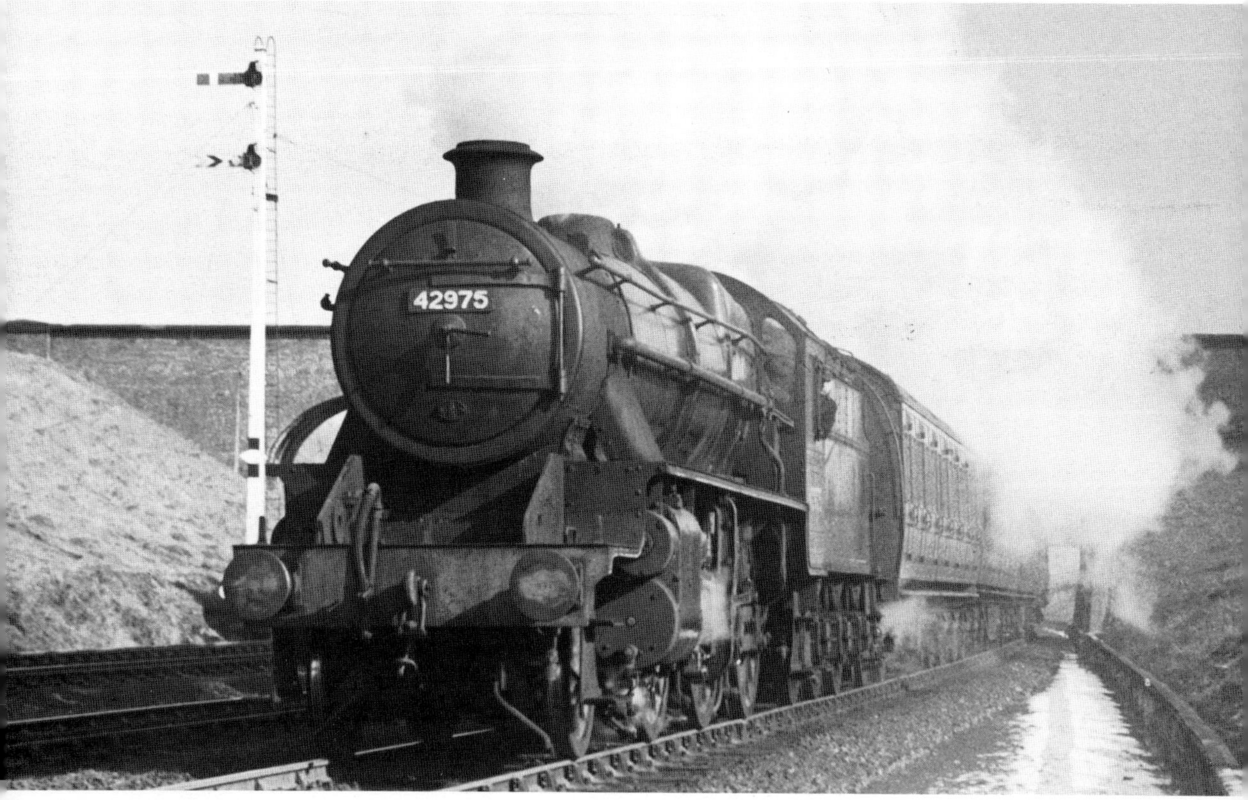
42975

*Left:* The ex-LMS Stanier 2-6-0 mixed traffic class of engine consisted of 40 members only and one of these No 42962 was photographed shunting in the goods yard by Chester General station on 1 August 1963. This picture clearly shows how much narrower the tender is than the engine.

*Below left:* Carrying no headlamp code of any kind a Stanier mixed traffic 2-6-0 No 42975 is seen running from Chester towards Saltney on 25 February 1956 with a train of empty coaching stock.

*Above:* On a spring day in 1955, a Fowler rebuild of Deeley ex-Midland Railway Class 3F 0-6-0 No 43809 has steam to spare as it climbs towards Acton Bridge with a Southbound loose coupled train of mineral wagons.

*Below:* A Stanier Class 8F 2-8-0 No 48462 passes Northwich station on 15 May 1965 at the head of a westbound loose coupled goods train. This station was once Cheshire Lines Committee property, the locomotive depot is on the right hand side of the picture and the goods yard in the left background.

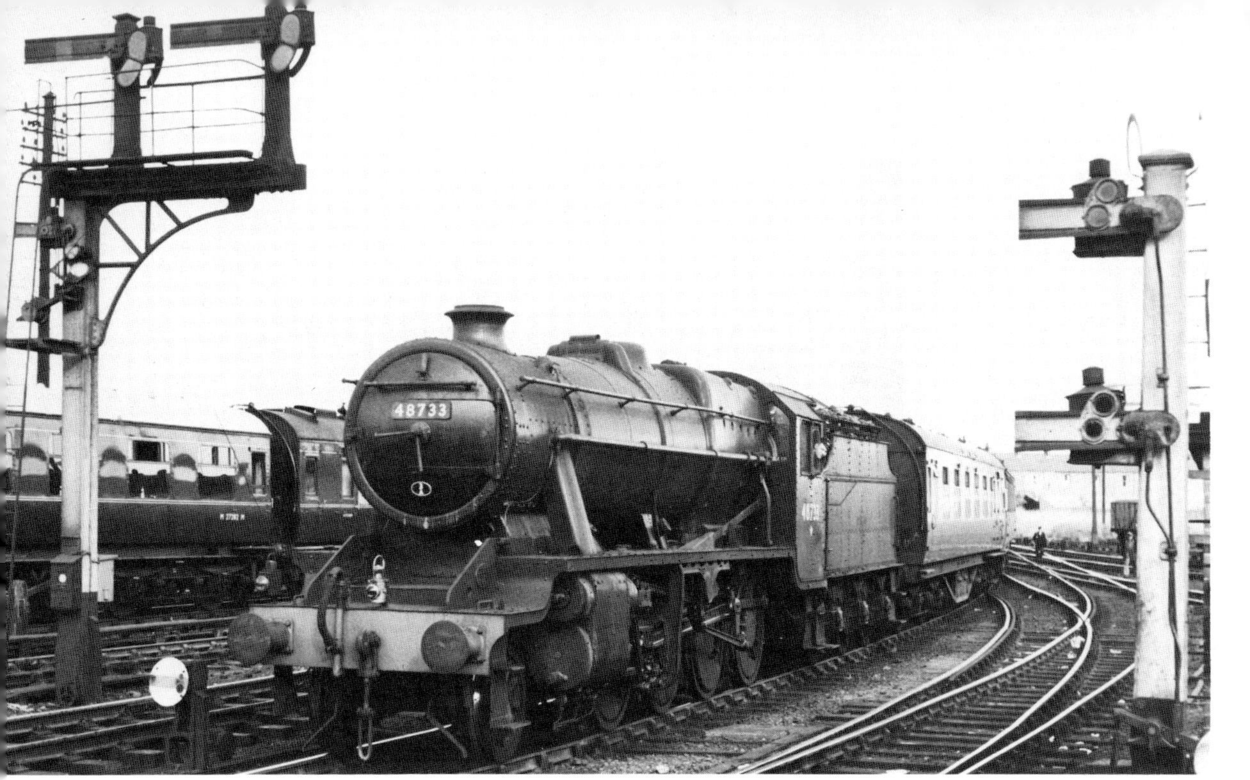
48733

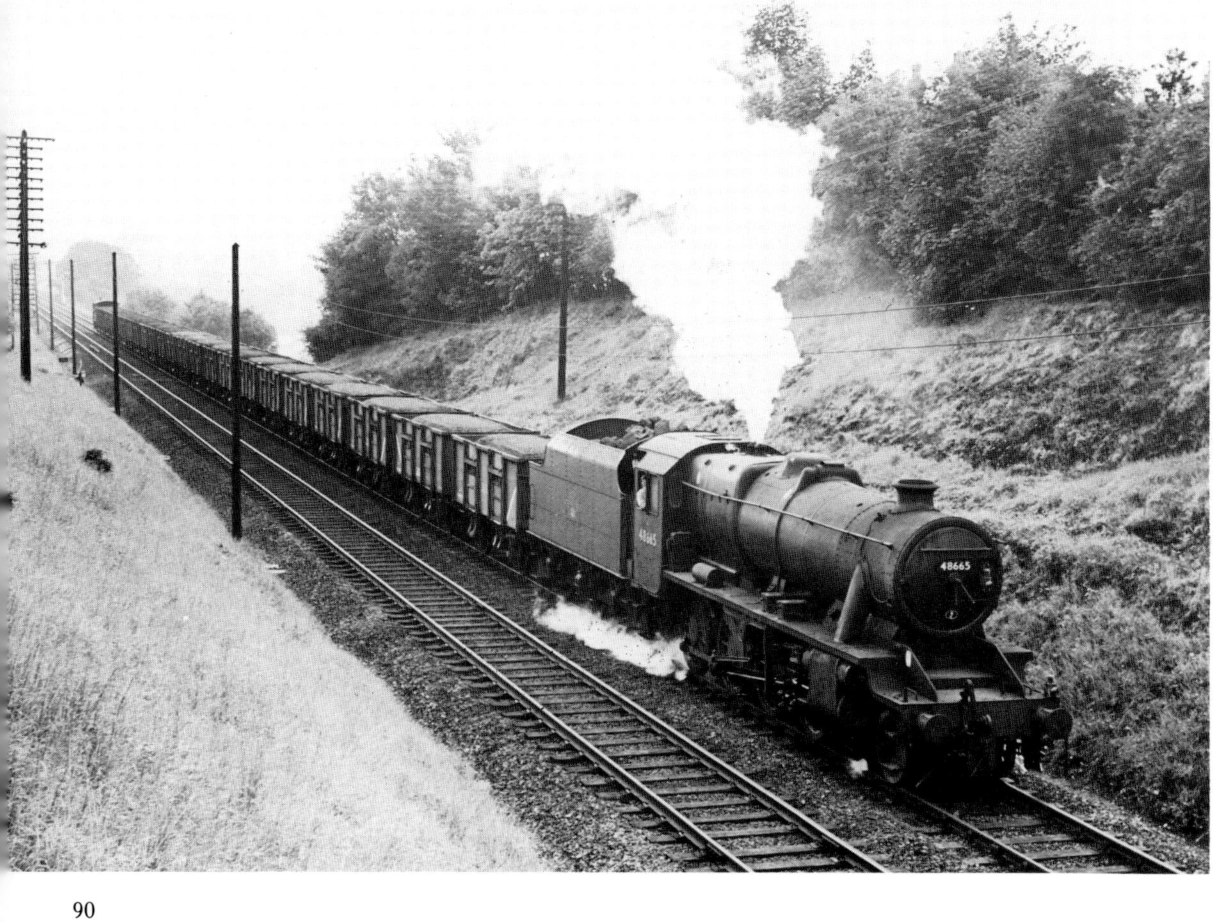
48665

*Above left:* In the late 1950s a number of Stanier Class 8F 2-8-0s acquired Fowler 3,500gal tenders. One of these engines No 48733 is seen running towards Chester General station on the down through line with a train of empty coaching stock on 15 August 1959.

*Left:* By the mid 1960s ex-Great Western steam locomotives had largely been replaced on the Chester to Shrewsbury main line by BR Standard types and Stanier 'Black 5s' and 8F 2-8-0s. One of the latter engines No 48665 is shown heading northwards towards Wrexham on 6 September 1965 with a train of loaded high capacity coal wagons from Bersham Colliery.

*Top:* Most of the goods trains passing Chester General station in an easterly direction used one of the through lines on the north side of the station. Here on 21 April 1965 a Stanier 8F 2-8-0 No 48090 is shown heading a mixed goods train from Birkenhead bound for the Warrington line.

*Above:* Still retaining a smokebox number plate with LMS style numerals, a Stanier Class 8F 2-8-0 No 48343 heads out from Chester on the down fast line towards Mold junction on 4 October 1957 with a train of ballast wagons.

*Above:* A Stanier Class 8F 2-8-0 No 48717 crosses the River Dee
bridge at Chester on 20 September 1957 with a down mixed
goods train past a Fowler 4F 0-6-0 No 44358, steaming towards
Chester with a goods train from Mold junction.

*Above right:* After being stopped at the signal gantry beyond the
road bridge in the background Stanier Class 5 No 45143 restarts
the 09.45 train from Penychain to Manchester Exchange
towards Platform 10 at Chester General station to make its
scheduled stop on 7 August 1965. Penychain was the station
built to serve Butlin's Holiday camp near to Pwllheli and the
train has travelled via Afon Wen and Bangor.

*Right:* On 19 June 1960 Stanier Class 5 No 44986 approaches
Chester with the 16.15 (Sundays only) Holyhead to Manchester
(Exchange). The engine is one of the later members of the class
with forward positioned top feed on the boiler and is running
coupled to one of the four coal weighing tenders which were
used with this class of engine to evaluate coal consumption.

*Above:* One of the Stanier Class 5s to be fitted with Caprotti valve gear No 44739 is seen running towards Platform 3 at Crewe station on 7 August 1958 with the 14.45 train from Llandudno. Signs of the forthcoming electrification are apparent with supporting masts for the catenary sprouting up here and there.

*Left:* The last two ex-LMS Class 5s were not completed until 1951, well into British Rail days, and were fitted with a revised form of Caprotti valve gear and detail differences including double chimney and higher running platform. The last of the two, No 44687 was photographed on 3 August 1959 hauling the Liverpool portion of the northbound 'Pines Express' towards Weaver junction and its next stop at Runcorn.

*Above:* It was rare for goods trains to be seen passing northwards through Crewe station, however on 19 September 1957, Stanier Class 5 No 45111 was seen heading along the down main through line with an assorted train of hopper wagons. The engine is one of the earlier series with a domeless boiler.

*Right:* As the ice cream salesman completes his sales by the first coach, Patricroft-based Stanier Class 5 No 45199 stands in Platform 4 at Chester General station ready to start with the 11.55 express from Manchester (Exchange) to Llandudno on a June Saturday in 1957. At this time the station had not been rebuilt and still retained its overall roof and low platforms.

*Above:* 5 June 1963 and a Stanier Class 5 No 45434 replenishes its tanks on one of the through goods lines at Chester General station. The footbridge which can be seen behind the signal gantry led to the station's Hoole Road entrance which had its own ticket barrier and booking office.

*Left:* Chester General station on 20 April 1965 and Stanier Class 5 No 45004 has just arrived at Platform 10 with the 09.15 express from Llandudno to London (Euston). The usual conference is taking place between the crew who have brought the train from North Wales and the relief men who will work the train on the final steam hauled part of its run to Crewe.